Letters on Kabbalah

Correspondences Between
Two Schools of Jewish Thought

Edited and Introduced by

J.J. Kimche

DA'AT PRESS

LETTERS ON KABBALAH

Correspondences Between Two Schools of Jewish Thought

First Edition, 2024

ISBN (Paperback): 9798852523730

www.daat.press / www.thehabura.com

THE SALOMON ZAGA RAYEK EDITION

דעת פרעס

DA'AT PRESS

Jewish books from the past, present, and future.

Explore more at www.daat.press

This book is lovingly dedicated to the memory of

Shlomo Moni ben Baluz זצ"ל

who emulated King Solomon in his relentless pursuit of goodness
and truth.

His life was a testament to the values captured in the verses:

ונתת לעבדך לב שומע לשפט את עמך להבין בין טוב לרע

*"Give Your servant an understanding heart to judge Your people and to discern
between good and evil."* (Kings I, 3:9)

His dedication to honesty and justice is mirrored in the verse:

ויאמר אלהים אליו יען אשר שאלת את הדבר הזה ושאלת לך הבין לשמוע משפט

*"Because you have asked for this and not for long life or wealth for yourself, nor
have asked for the death of your enemies, but for discernment in administering
justice."* (Kings I, 3:11)

His wisdom resonates with the words:

הנה נתתי לך לב חכם ונבון

"I will do what you have asked. I will give you a wise and discerning heart."
(Kings I, 3:12)

These virtues of **Shlomo Moni ben Baluz זצ"ל** have been a
guiding force for our family.

It is our hope that this book will enlighten all of Am Yisrael in
their journey towards understanding their mission in this world,
always remembering that ראשית חכמה יראת ה'

Contents

Introduction & Context

Introduction & Context

J.J. Kimche, Editor

1: Conflicting Narratives

Is Kabbalah a central pillar of the Jewish religion? Do the structures, symbols, and texts at the heart of Kabbalah represent an ancient mystical core of the Jewish tradition? Can they be conceived as the authentic significance submerged within Judaism's canonical texts? Or are they merely a later invention, a fanciful medieval theology, an alien interloper whose ideas are profoundly at odds with more authoritative streams of Judaism?

This nest of questions has bedevilled students of this topic for centuries. To this day, Kabbalah remains a subject of curiosity and controversy precisely because its story may be told in two wildly divergent ways.

The first version of this story is the one which is relayed by its adherents, who maintain that there is no Judaism – indeed, no true knowledge of the One God –

without the doctrines and symbols of Kabbalah. It is thus fitting that the biblical Adam, into whose body the vivifying breath of God was infused, was also initiated into a body of knowledge, both secret and foundational (the word *Sod* in Hebrew denotes both), containing the concealed truths regarding God and His creation. This body of mystical doctrines and symbols were henceforth relayed through the generations of biblical personae, including the great patriarchs, prophets, and leaders who populate the pantheon of Israel's biblical religion. Given that the contents of Kabbalah were known to the great protagonists and authors of the biblical books, it stands to reason that they are also encoded throughout the length and breadth of the Hebrew Bible, as prophets from Moses to Malakhi covertly interlaced the secrets of Kabbalah within their writings. It is therefore the case that these mystical secrets constitute the *Tanakh*'s deepest stratum of significance, imbuing even the most pedestrian of biblical passages with dimensions of incalculable divine profundity.

Kabbalah, however, did not end with the canonisation of the Hebrew Bible. Judaism's body of secret knowledge, according to this narrative, also pulsates beneath and within rabbinic literature. Cryptic hints towards esoteric teachings and practices – such as the body of forbidden knowledge referred to as the 'Narrative of Genesis' *(ma'ase bereshit)* and 'Narrative of the Chariot'[1] *(ma'ase merkaba)*, or episodes of mystical peregrinations such as the 'four who entered the orchard'[2] – are to be interpreted as references not simply to esoteric material as such, but rather to ancient forms of Kabbalah. In a similar vein, the vast reservoir of *aggadah*, the peculiarly rabbinic form of folkloric and anecdotal narratives scattered across Talmudic and Midrashic anthologies, constitute fertile soil for the development of Kabbalistic themes and speculations.

While the senior rabbinic figures of the Mishnah and the Talmud, according to this narrative, were all adherents of Kabbalah, there was one sage in particular who was principally responsible for its coalescence and transmission under difficult historical circumstances. Rabbi Shimon bar Yoḥai (often known by his acronym RaSHb"Y) lived in the Land of Israel during the Roman persecutions of the second century. Through years of self-seclusion, he contemplated, formulated, and

---

[1] These terms are referred to as מעשה בראשית and מעשה מרכבה in rabbinic tradition, and according to a Mishnaic tradition, are forbidden to be taught in public. See: Mishna, *Ḥagigah* 2:1; BT *Ḥagigah* 13a, JT *Ḥagigah* 2:1.

[2] This legend is related in: Tosefta, *Ḥagigah*, 2:2; BT *Ḥagigah* 14a; JT *Ḥagigah* 2:1.

crystallised the major principles of Kabbalah, and succeeded in passing on this knowledge to a few select disciples, including his son Ele'azar, prior to his death. The conversations and activities of RaSHb"Y and the rest of his *Ḥevrayah* (circle of disciples) were recorded verbatim and written down as a series of texts, published later in the *Sefer Ha-Zohar* (or 'book of illuminations'). It is this extraordinary mystical compendium, whose theological, legal, and eschatological statements have exerted a massively disproportionate influence within Jewish history, which would eventually emerge as the constitutional text of the Kabbalistic tradition.

Of course, even after its transcription and dissemination, the Zohar remained part of a deeply esoteric discipline. Hidden from the public gaze, only small circles of mystical initiates in each generation were privy to its enchanted inner cosmos. It was in this oral, esoteric form that the Zohar and its attendant teachings were passed down for over a millennium, until the 12th and 13th centuries CE, during which some Kabbalists began to break their silence and commit a portion of their recondite knowledge to writing. This process reached its pinnacle during the final decades of the 1200s, during which a Spanish Kabbalist by the name of Moses de Leon (c. 1240-1305) began to transcribe and publish

14

the literary centrepiece of Kabbalah, namely the Zohar. The dissemination of this work over the following centuries precipitated a renaissance of Kabbalistic scholarship and illumination, as clusters of scholars across the Jewish world sought to clarify, crystallise, and embellish the system of ideas laid out in the Kabbalistic canon. This process culminated in the works of the most authoritative of the early modern Kabbalists, such as the great systematiser Moses Qordobero (RaMa"Q, 1522-1570) and the prodigious theological innovator Isaac Luria (ArIza"l, 1534-1572). Such pivotal figures in turn laid the groundwork for the works of the Hasidic thinkers and other modern Kabbalists, who must be considered the legitimate heirs of the immortal chain of Kabbalistic mysticism.

According to its adherents, therefore, Kabbalah fulfils the three major criteria of legitimacy: antiquity, authenticity, and authority. In their eyes, Kabbalah possesses the same *antiquity* as humanity itself, the same *authenticity* as the oral Torah, and comparable *authority* to the system of Halakhah by which religious Jews live their lives. This is the traditional account of Kabbalah – and it is to some version of this story that a majority of observant Jews have adhered for centuries, including the lion's share of Orthodox Jewry today.

More critically-minded readers, however, will ascribe an entirely different history to Kabbalistic texts and ideas.[3] Members of this second group, and especially those who have engaged with the massive profusion of academic scholarship on the history of Kabbalah[4] available to the general public since 1840, will object to almost all the elements of the narrative recounted by the first group, as outlined above. True, the irreducible

---

[3] I should perhaps clarify that 'critical' in this sense does not necessarily imply the adoption of an adverse approach to Kabbalah itself. Indeed, there were some enthusiastic exponents of Kabbalah who have endorsed and assimilated the critical, namely academic, scholarship on the subject. One such example was the maverick Israeli *Rosh Yeshiba*, Rabbi Menachem Froman (1945-2013), who taught Kabbalah as a religious discipline yet interwove the latest academic research into his classes on the subject. I am grateful to Mordy Miller, of Ben-Gurion University, for pointing this out to me.

[4] The classic introduction to the ideas of Kabbalah, used now by generations of students, is Gershom Scholem's *Major Trends in Jewish Mysticism* (Schocken, 1941, republished 2011). Although somewhat dated, this book is still of immense utility, especially for students who prefer a historical approach to the subject. For those who favour a phenomenological approach, Moshe Hallamish's *An Introduction to the Kabbalah* (State University New York Press, 1999) is the best introductory work in English. Joseph Dan's *Kabbalah: A Very Short Introduction* (Oxford University Press, 2007) also deserves an honourable mention as an admirably concise yet thorough guide to this labyrinthine topic.

presence of religious mysticism[5] within the development of Judaism must be acknowledged, as must the existence of various forms of Jewish mysticism that are reflected in the texts of Judaism's ancient and early medieval period. Yet partisans of this second narrative will also draw a sharp distinction between these many strains of mysticism that are reflected (often in a fragmentary and cryptic manner) in earlier texts – such as the Mishnah, Talmud, Apocrypha and Pseudepigrapha, Qumran Scrolls, Merkabah and Hekhalot literature, and the writings of Philo[6] – on the one hand, and Kabbalah on the other. Put otherwise, the term 'Kabbalah', although incorporating many themes and techniques from these earlier strands of Judaic mysticism, actually consists of a

---

[5] Mysticism is a notoriously slippery term, with oceans of ink having been spilled in the vain hope of providing a fully satisfactory account of this commonly used and abused term. Without being so presumptuous as to believe that I have solved this lexicographical and philosophical conundrum, it seems that the following fairly loose definition of religious mysticism may be useful for our present purposes: religious mysticism is a set of ideas and practices through which a religious devotee seeks apprehension of, and communion with, a divine or metaphysical dimension of existence, usually via the medium of finely honed emotional, spiritual, and instinctual faculties.

[6] A good survey of this early emergence of mysticism is Peter Schäfer, *The origins of Jewish mysticism* (Princeton University Press, 2011).

set of very specific doctrines[7] that emerged during the twelfth and thirteenth centuries.

So, according to this critical approach, how did Kabbalah arise?[8] As far as we can tell from the rather parsimonious textual evidence, the birthplace of this new form of theosophical speculation was the Provençal region during the twelfth century. This remarkably productive and literate Jewish community in southern France was an epicentre of the controversy surrounding the works of Moses Maimonides (RaMBa"M, 1138-1204), whose fervently rationalist, neo-Aristotelian interpretation of central tenets of Judaism caused considerable consternation among his traditionally-

---

[7] It must be noted that three separate although interlinked forms of Kabbalah emerged in the late medieval period. The theosophical-theurgic school of Kabbalah (centred around the Zohar); the prophetic-ecstatic school of Kabbalah (centred around the teachings of Abraham Abulafia); and the practical-magical tradition of Kabbalah, which seeks to alter the world through occult practices and mantic techniques. For more on this, see: Moshe Idel, *Hasidism: Between Ecstasy and Magic* (State University of New York Press, 1995), idem. Seeing as the first of these schools of Kabbalah has achieved primacy during recent centuries, it is this strand that will be the focus of this essay.

[8] A concise yet illuminating overview of pre-Zoharic Kabbalah can be found in: Arthur Green, *A Guide to the Zohar* (Stanford University Press, 2004), p. 9-60.

minded rabbinic colleagues, especially within the more culturally insular communities of Medieval Ashkenaz.[9]

In the eyes of these latter scholars, especially the Western European rabbis who were heirs to French and Rheinish traditions, Maimonides' teachings – particularly those regarding an entirely de-personified deity, the intellectualisation of the Torah's commandments, and the naturalisation of all miracles – were unconscionable. Their far more 'enchanted' view

---

[9] It must be noted here that there exists a broad spectrum, both within the academic and rabbinic world, as to the precise nature of Maimonides' Aristotelian sympathies. On one side of the spectrum lies Leo Strauss and his followers, who viewed Maimonides as an orthodox Aristotelian garbed in a cloak of rabbinic devotion and piety. (See, for instance: Kenneth Hart Green, Ed., *Leo Strauss on Maimonides: The Complete Writings* (University of Chicago Press, 2013)). The other side of the spectrum is occupied by more traditionalist scholars such as Rabbi Dr. Jose Faur (see: *Homo Mysticus: A Guide to Maimonides's Guide for the Perplexed* (Syracuse University Press: 1999)), who see Maimonides' Guide as a philosophically-oriented presentation of traditional, even mystically-inclined, ideas that were already firmly entrenched within the Sepharadi intellectual tradition. An eminently plausible middle position – namely, that while Maimonides was deeply rooted and strongly influenced by Islamic Neo-Aristotelianism, he departs from it on a number of significant epistemological and theological issues – has been ably defended by Kenneth Seeskin in his article in the SEP. See: Seeskin, Kenneth, "Maimonides", *The Stanford Encyclopedia of Philosophy* (Spring 2021), Edward N. Zalta (ed.), URL: plato.stanford.edu/archives/spr2021/entries/maimonides

of Judaism, including elements of folk magic, mystical speculations, and the use of divine names to effect change in the universe, had to be vigorously defended and reformulated. As with many intellectual pendulums, a wild swing in one direction precipitated an equally wild swing in the other. Thus, it was precisely in the eye of the Maimonidean storm[10] that anti-rationalist scholars began to formulate a series of mystical doctrines concerning the great metaphysical conundrums that perturbed all serious religious thinkers of the medieval period. Such thorny issues included the nature of God's essence; the mechanisms behind creation; the content and purpose of revelation; the presence of evil; and the ultimate purpose of humankind.

Foremost among these issues was the tension between the apparently simultaneous doctrines of divine immanence and transcendence. How can the unimaginable, indescribable, entirely abstract Deity posited by the philosophers be reconciled with the

---

[10] This theory that Kabbalah arose in large part as a response to the excesses of Jewish rationalism has been propounded by Moshe Idel and endorsed by Menachem Kellner. See: Moshe Idel, 'Maimonides and Kabbalah', in Isadore Twersky (ed.), *Studies in Maimonides* (Harvard University Press, 1990), 31-81; Menachem Kellner, *Maimonides' Confrontation with Mysticism* (Liverpool University Press, 2006), p. 1-10.

communicative, personified, and exquisitely attentive God described in the bible? And how can this ultimately indivisible unity have brought forth such fractious and flawed multiplicity?[11]

In consonance with regnant Neo-Platonic ideas of their era,[12] medieval Kabbalists chose to bridge this chasm through describing ten emanations, or stages of manifestation, through which the divine brought about the created world. These ten stages are described by early Kabbalists through all sorts of metaphors, such as 'names', 'utterances', 'crowns', 'qualities', or 'principles', yet as Kabbalah progressed through the thirteenth and fourteenth centuries, the term *Sefirot* (literally: 'numbers') came to be the dominant appellation employed for describing this ten-stage process. The ten *Sefirot*, or stages of emanation, also came to be identified

---

[11] These following paragraphs describing the *Sefirot* has been lifted, with some minor revisions, from the "Glossary of Kabbalistic Terms", an appendix to my forthcoming translation and elucidation of Shadal's "Dialogue Concerning the Wisdom of the Kabbalah, The Antiquity of the Zohar, and the Antiquity of the Vowelisation and Cantillation Marks", projected publication 2024, Palgrave Macmillan.

[12] For a wide-ranging and high-quality set of essays on the interaction between medieval Judaism and Neo-Platonism, see: Lenn E. Goodman, ed., *Neo-Platonism and Jewish thought* (State University of New York Press, 2012).

as the fundamental attributes of divinity that were made manifest in the creation of the universe. It became the central endeavour of various Kabbalistic authors to describe the manner in which a well-trained mystic, through aligning themselves with the divine frameworks symbolised by the structures and interactions of the *Sefirot*, could achieve communion with God.

Prior to these emanations, all that existed was the **En Sof** – that is, the divine essence in its pure, inexpressible, transcendental state, closely analogous to Aristotle's First Cause or Plotinus' the One. It existed in a state of sublime unity and aloneness, as nothing could co-exist with or interrupt its infinitude. In order to create, the Divine had to contract itself, through a process called *Ṣimṣum*, in order to allow for other entities to come into being. The first of these entities to emanate from the pure divine essence is the first and highest of the *Sefirot*, generally called **Keter** (crown). Although sometimes indistinguishable from the *En Sof* itself, *Keter* is usually seen as the first point from which existence itself flowed forth from the *En Sof*. Emanating from *Keter* are the two subsequent *Sefirot* – **Hokhmah** (wisdom) and **Binah** (understanding). *Hokhmah* is usually portrayed as an active, masculine flow of divine wisdom, which is in turn accepted by *Binah*, the representation of Mother Wisdom, which gives birth to the subsequent seven Sefirot. These first three *Sefirot* constitute a triad representing the superconscious and conscious aspects of the divine mind or will, from which all subsequent entities result.

The next triad in the Sefirotic sequence begins with the antithetical archetypes **Ḥesed** (grace) and **Geburah** (power), which reach their full expression in their synthesis **Tiferet** (glory).[13] This triad represents the balancing forces of God's masculine, merciful side (*Ḥesed*) and his demanding, feminine side (*Geburah*), and finally their ideal equilibrium (*Tiferet*). The next triad consists of **Neṣaḥ** (eternity), **Hod** (splendour), and their synthesis **Yesod** (foundation). It is through this latter *Sefirah* that all the divine forces converge in their desired equipoise and stand poised to pulsate through existence as a coherent, creative force. Creativity *in potentia*, however, was insufficient. The creation of a tangible world required a receptacle, a channel through which the boundless potency of the divine emanations may be concretised. This is the role of the tenth and final stage, that of **Malkhut** (kingdom or royalty), which both

---

[13] In medieval Kabbalistic literature, this *Sefirah* is frequently called *Raḥamim* (compassion).

receives and gives corporeal form to the entire creative process, allowing for the instantiation of a physical realm that is suffused with divine presence. It is for this reason that the final *Sefirah* is also identified with **Shekhinah**, God's indwelling presence, as well as with God's creative speech-act (sometimes analogised to the divine *Logos*). The relationship between *Yesod* and *Malkhut* is often depicted in terms of sexual congress, as the divine flow emanates from *Yesod* (which corresponds to the male member, belonging ultimately to the male figure embodied by *Tiferet*) and embeds itself fruitfully within the feminine channel of *Malkhut*, eventually producing a created world.

This ten-staged structure of the *Sefirot* has proved endlessly productive. It has been invested with endless symbolic dimensions, as generations of Kabbalists have expended oceans of ink identifying each of these ten stages to, *inter alia*, the human body, limbs of a tree, forces of nature, stages of human development, psychological processes, celestial bodies, and biblical protagonists. Most importantly, the *Sefirot* constitute a chain of causation that connects the inexpressible divine essence to the concrete physical world, thus satisfying the initial theological quandary by positing both a transcendent and immanent aspect to the divine realm.

While functioning as a bridge across this theological chasm, the Sefirot have been alternately understood as both part of the divine being itself yet also part of its creation.[14] Fully aware of the theological trip-wires, Kabbalists generally display a certain reticence regarding the precise nature of the relationship between the *En Sof* and the rest of the *Sefirot*. Various metaphors have been formulated to this end, the most arresting of which – "like a flame attached to an ember" – reflects the subtly required to describe two entities that are simultaneously connected and separate. While hewing to both sides of this delicate ambiguity, Kabbalists can speak of multiple aspects of the divine (and justify anthropomorphic representations of God in the bible), all the while venerating the transcendence and unity of the *En Sof*.

An important consequence of the Sefirotic framework is the theurgic power that became attributed to human actions. According to many Kabbalists, due to the sins of human beings (or perhaps due to a cosmic malfunction that occurred during creation), the *Sefirot*

---

[14] In fact, there is a lively debate among medieval Kabbalists as to whether these ten *Sefirot* ought to be understood as part of the divine essence itself, or merely as divine vessels that were created in a fashion similar to everything else. This issue is roughly analogous to Christological debates about the co-eternality of Christ.

exist in a state of disharmony and disrepair (**Shebirah**), internally ruptured and externally alienated from one another. It is for this reason that the **Sitra Aḥra** ('other side'), the spiritual forces of evil, are able to cause damage and pain in the physical realm. It is therefore the task of human beings, through the punctilious performance of good deeds and execution of religious ritual, to bring about the rectification, or **Tiqqun**, of the supernal realms. Through reuniting and repairing the *Sefirot* and their errant 'sparks', the actions of even the humblest Jew may help restore harmony to the cosmos, thereby hastening the final, eschatological state of harmony in both the upper and lower realms.

This framework of Kabbalistic doctrines outlined in the preceding paragraphs – despite the objections levelled by generations of erudite detractors – constitutes an intellectually fertile, symbologically powerful, and theologically imaginative version of Judaic religion. Through reimagining the divine realm not as a static unity but rather as a teeming, vivified ecosystem of supernal potentialities emanating from an indescribable Singularity, the Kabbalists effectively bridged the gap between the transcendent and immanent conceptions of God, in addition to adumbrating a philosophically respectable (at least to the medieval imagination) account of creation. The titanic struggles between these divine forces allow for an account of evil and imbalance within the created world, while the imperative of *Tiqqun* both in the heavens and on earth provides a compelling rationale for the performance of the Torah's commandments, however great or small. In their response to (the excesses of?) philosophical rationalism, Jewish mystics succeeded in formulating an entirely novel yet traditionally reverberative conception of some of the most basic facets of their religion. It is Kabbalah's radical novelty, its undisguisable dissimilarities to the major thrust of biblical and the rabbinic theology,[15] which lies at the centre of the anti-Kabbalistic critique.

Of course, such an intricate chain of esoteric doctrines could hardly have been formulated overnight. After its initial flowering in Provence, the centre of Kabbalistic activity moved across the Pyrenees into the Iberian Peninsula, which until the previous century stood as the global hub of Jewish intellectual and cultural activity. One new important centre of Kabbalah was the

---

[15] It must be admitted that several defenders of Kabbalah have countered this point by arguing that the rationalistic theology of Maimonides and his school constitutes an even greater innovation within the history of Jewish thought. Such a critique undoubtedly contains at least a grain of validity, yet it remains far beyond the scope of this introduction.

region of Catalonia, in which the monumental figure of Moses Naḥmanides (RaMBa"N, 1194-1270) lent his considerable authority to establishing the credence of Kabbalistic doctrines.[16] While Naḥmanides, in the spirit of a true mystic, remained highly circumspect when discussing mystical subjects, his Gironese colleagues Rabbi Ezra and Rabbi Azriel were far more verbose, composing some of the first extensive commentaries explicitly outlining the doctrines of the *Sefirot*.

Yet it was not Catalonia, but rather its western counterpart Castile, that would become the more famous and influential centre of Kabbalistic thought. The years between 1280-1310 witnessed a resurgence of mythically-inclined Kabbalistic speculation among the writings of a phenomenally creative circle of mystics, including Joseph Gikatilla, Joseph Angelet, Todros Abulafia, and, most significantly of all, Moses de Leon (c.1240-1305). It was the collective adventures – philosophical, hermeneutical, and experiential – of this circle that produced a mesmerising anthology of Kabbalistic tales, musings, traditions, sermons, and

---

[16] While historians generally try to avoid counterfactual speculation, it seems fairly safe to conclude that without the decisive endorsement of Naḥmanides and his followers, Kabbalistic ideas may never have broken into mainstream rabbinic circles.

discourses. This corpus, initially transcribed and disseminated by Moshe de Leon between the years 1285-1300, eventually became known collectively as the Zohar, and assumed its place as *the* canonical text within the Kabbalistic tradition.[17] True, Kabbalah has developed in wildly different directions since the year 1300, with the Lurianic, Sabbatean, and Ḥasidic movements all inaugurating new directions in the history of Jewish mysticism. Yet, on a broadly substantive level, Kabbalah rests upon the authority of the Zohar – the legitimacy of which has come under severe scrutiny ever since its very inception.

This, therefore, is the crux of the debate regarding Kabbalah. Those who subscribe to the critical approach outlined above will inevitably advance the

---

[17] The precise manner in which the Zohar came to be written in the late thirteenth century has been the subject of intense debate among historians in recent decades. Some, like Gershom Scholem, have seen the Zohar as the almost exclusive product of the fertile mind and pen of Moses de Leon, whereas more recent scholars, such as Ronit Meroz, understand the Zohar as a far more fragmented text that had been collated over several generations. I have here described and endorsed a middle position, namely that the vast portion of the Zoharic text was the product of a specific circle of Castilian Kabbalists, of which de Leon was their principal literary agent. Such a theory has been proposed by Yehuda Liebes, perhaps the greatest living authority on the subject. See: Yehuda Liebes, *Studies in the Zohar* (State University New York Press, 1993), pp. 85-138.

29

claim that Kabbalah – and specifically its central text, the Zohar – passes none of the three criteria of legitimacy posited earlier. First, it has no legitimate claim of *antiquity*. Rather, it must be conceived as a radical innovation within the history of Jewish ideas, arising in the late medieval period largely as a reaction to competing ideological strains. Second, it is not *authentic*, in the sense that it cannot claim to constitute an unbroken *Kabbalah* (literally: 'tradition') from time immemorial. That this body of doctrines has much in common with non-Jewish intellectual traditions such as Gnosticism and Neo-Platonism further undermines Kabbalah's pretensions as an autochthonous strand of Judaism. Finally, by dint of its relatively late innovation, Kabbalah cannot claim anything like the kind of *legitimacy* assumed by the texts that form the backbone of the Jewish canon. Its daringly novel theological structures, legal statements, and hermeneutic techniques stand in stark opposition to the unimpeachable, venerable elements of the Jewish faith, as found in biblical and rabbinic literature. Therefore, all attempts to mould Jewish beliefs and practices along Kabbalistic contours must be resisted as a matter of principle.

This, in brief, is the crux of the argument surrounding Kabbalah: two staunchly opposing narratives, each with their own account of Kabbalah's origins and significance, and each defended by fierce proponents stretching back 700 years.

2: A History of Kabbalah Criticism

Some will advance the argument that this debate is now entirely moot. After all, recent centuries of Jewish history appear to have decided overwhelmingly in favour of Kabbalah and the Zohar. It certainly remains beyond doubt that Kabbalah has successfully integrated itself into the theology, religious rituals, and folk practices of Jewish communities worldwide. Indeed, so successful has been the interweaving of Kabbalistic dogma and praxis within mainstream Judaism that many contemporary Jews are entirely unaware, indeed would be baffled at the very suggestion, of a Judaism without Kabbalah. In the minds of many practitioners of Judaism today, the legitimacy of Kabbalah and the authenticity of the Zohar are as inviolably axiomatic as any other article of faith. Yet this extraordinary success belies an important yet vastly under-appreciated intellectual tradition: that of Kabbalah criticism across the centuries. It is to this quasi-taboo element of Jewish intellectual history that we must now turn.

Scepticism, even hostility, towards Kabbalah and the Zohar accompanied the emergence of the phenomenon itself. Prior to the cataclysmic expulsion of Spanish Jewry in 1492, Kabbalistic ideas circulated through the Jewish world in a gradual, partial, and clandestine manner. Yet even during this seminal stage, in which only a minute proportion of Jewish scholars would have engaged with these ideas, pockets of resistance flared up almost immediately. The earliest significant source we have for this is the private writings of the fourteenth century Kabbalist Isaac of Acre, whose testimony was eventually published in an early sixteenth century historical collection titled *Sefer Yuḥasin*.[18] This text relays an episode that occurred in the year 1305, a

---

[18] Isaac of Acre's testimony was published in the first edition of the *Sefer Yuḥasin*, printed in Constantinople in 1566, although it was excised from subsequent editions due to its controversial nature. The fullest version of this passage can be found in *Sefer Yuḥasin Ha-Shalem* (London and Edinburgh, 1857, p. 88-89). Isaiah Tishby, in the introduction to his extraordinary anthology *The Wisdom of the Zohar: An Anthology of Texts*, (Transl. David Goldstein, Liverpool University Press, 1989, p. 28-29) reproduces Isaac of Acre's testimony in full. While scholars of Kabbalah have differed regarding the extent to which this testimony is historically reliable and useful regarding the specific question of authorship, it unquestionably reflects the existence of strong Zohar skepticism in the years immediately following the initial dissemination of Zoharic texts.

period in which the earliest sections of Zoharic corpus were beginning to be disseminated among mystical circles in Spain and the Land of Israel. According to Isaac of Acre, rabbinic authorities in Spain were sharply divided regarding the authenticity and authority of the Zohar, with many expressing their doubts that this text was authored by a Mishnaic sage, or that it contained authentic expressions of Jewish theology. Having met Moses de Leon himself, Isaac of Acre decided to travel to the former's hometown in order to visit the ancient manuscript from which Moses de Leon claimed to have copied down his Zoharic writings. By the time Isaac arrived, however, Moses de Leon had passed away. Isaac promptly turned to de Leon's widow and offered her a substantial settlement in return for this ancient manuscript. To his disappointment, de Leon's widow, in a statement confirmed by her daughter, refused his offer point blank. She stated that there was no such ancient manuscript, and that her husband had authored these texts entirely of his own accord. When she pressed her husband on this point, de Leon apparently responded that he only claimed the Zoharic texts to be ancient in order to secure their authority and his own fortune. From this testimony of his wife and daughter, Isaac of

Acre claimed, we see that the Zohar was none other than the product of de Leon's vivid imagination.

Isaac of Acre's testimony constitutes a valuable contemporaneous account that provides two crucial pieces of evidence. First, that Moses de Leon did not copy the Zoharic texts from any ancient manuscript, but rather relied on his own quite remarkable creativity. Second, that from the moment the Zoharic texts began to circulate, many learned authorities were convinced that these texts were modern fabrications. Isaac of Acre's testimony, once published in 1566, became a cornerstone of the historical case against the Zohar, one that would be cited repeatedly by opponents of the Kabbalah.

Quite aside from Isaac of Acre's personal reminiscence, there is a small cache of textual evidence noting a sense of unease regarding central Kabbalistic ideas, as they began to seep into mainstream rabbinic circles. Such unease is reflected in the highly influential legal responsa of Isaac ben Sheshet Perfet (the RiBa"SH, 1326-1408), in which he casts aspersions upon the Kabbalistic notion of directing one's intentions towards specific *Sefirot* during the daily prayers:

Also, in the prayer of the eighteen benedictions [The Kabbalists] have a specific Sefirah towards which they direct their intentions for each and every different blessing. All this is exceedingly bizarre in my eyes, as one who is not a Kabbalist like them. There are those who believe this to be a polytheistic doctrine, and I have already heard one of the philosophically-inclined scholars denigrate the Kabbalists, saying that 'the idolaters [i.e., Christians] believe in three gods, whereas the kabbalists believe in ten gods.'[19]

While it is true that the RiBa"SH receives an answer to his quandaries from a Kabbalist, he remains far from satisfied, as he reiterates towards the end of that very same responsum.

Thus was the explanation of the aforementioned pious one regarding the intentions of the Kabbalists, and it is very satisfactory. However, who invited us into all this? Surely it is better to pray directly and intently to God, and He will know how best to satisfy the request, as the verse states 'commit your way to God, trust in him and he will do this.' (Psalms 37:5). Thus said the great teacher Shimshon De-Kinnon

---

[19] *Responsa of the RiBa"SH*, Question 157 (Jerusalem, 1993, p.34a in the Hebrew pagination).

whom I mentioned above. Similarly, I have informed you what my master, my teacher, Rabbenu Nissim said to me, that the RaMBa"N himself was far too mired within Kabbalistic beliefs.

The point being made by the RiBa"SH, through the mouth of his philosophically-minded colleague, is that the Kabbalists' portrayal of a Divinity manifest through ten hypostatic stages appears very similar to the Christian trinitarian belief, which much of the rabbinic tradition has deemed idolatrous.

Interestingly, it was precisely this accusation that was levelled by Abraham Abulafia, one of the most important (non-Zoharic) Kabbalists of the thirteenth century, in a famous letter to Rabbi Shelomo ben Aderet (RaSHb"A, 1235-1310). Abulafia asserts those who believe in the doctrine of the *Sefirot* "differ only slightly from Christians, seeing as they substitute the trinity for a ten-part structure, which they identify with God".[20]

---

[20] The letter in question was published in full by Adolf Jellinek, in his *Auswahl Kabbalistischer Mystik* (Leipzig, 1853) Part I, p.13. For Rashba's response to Abulafia, see his Responsa 548 (Vienna, 1812, 71b-72b). For a broader analysis of this epistolary controversy, see: M. Idel, "The Rashba and Abraham Abulafia: The Story of an Ignored Kabbalistic Polemic," in: *Atara l'Haim: Studies in the Talmud and Medieval Rabbinic Literature in Honour of Professor Haim Zalman*

This discomfort with central Kabbalistic doctrines and texts even among Kabbalists themselves is confirmed by a brief aside by Joseph ibn Wakar, a fourteenth century authority within mystical circles. In his *Shorshe Ha-Kabbalah* ('Roots of Tradition'), ibn Wakar lists a range of reliable Kabbalistic texts, whose ideas are representative of Judaism's true mystical teachings. With regards to the Zohar, however, he insists that "it is necessary [for the reader] to be careful... for there occur in this book very many errors. Therefore, it is necessary to be careful and keep within bounds from it."[21] Such fragments of testimony, while hardly overwhelming, are certainly sufficient to establish the fact that the acceptance of Zoharic Kabbalah – even among Kabbalistic circles – was hardly a foregone conclusion.

Yet, the spread of the Kabbalah continued apace. The sixteenth century, with its political upheavals, demographic shifts, and technological advances, was the seminal era that witnessed the dramatic spread of

---

Dimitrovsky, ed. Daniel Boyarin, et. al. (Magnes Press, 2000), pp. 235-51.

[21] Joseph b. Abraham Ibn Waqar, *Principles of the Qabbalah*, edited from Hebrew and Arabic Manuscripts, by P. B. Fenton (Cherub Press, 2004), p. 122. The translation is taken from Scholem's *Major Trends*, (p. 394, note 124), who translated directly from the manuscript source (124 Ms. Vatican, 203, f. 63b).

Kabbalistic texts and teachings. The dispersion of Spanish Jewry throughout the world following their expulsion in 1492 was certainly a major contributing factor. It has been argued, with reasonable plausibility, that the historical and theological categories of Kabbalah were well-equipped to ascribe religious significance to the traumatic experiences of rupture and dislocation, and was therefore adopted by expellees and *conversos* as a kind of psychological-religious defence mechanism.[22] Kabbalah also benefited from the lamentable decline of rationalist Jewish philosophy in the fourteenth and fifteenth centuries, and found a more hospitable climate for its ideas among the burgeoning Jewish communities within the Ottoman Empire and the Polish-Lithuanian commonwealth.

However, the principal factor that enabled the spread and acceptance of Kabbalah was the emergence of printing. It was this transformative technology which allowed for the Zohar, as well as other central works of Kabbalah, to be disseminated with unprecedented speed

---

[22] This is the subject of an argument between Gershom Scholem (who maintained that the Lurianic school of Kabbalah arose as a theological reaction to the 1492 expulsion) and Moshe Idel, who disputes this. See: Scholem, *Trends*, p. 193-221; Moshe Idel, *Kabbalah: New Perspectives*, (Yale University Press, 1988) p.256-267.

and efficiency. Indeed, it was only with its printing in Cremona and Mantua during the 1550s that the Zohar ceased to be a loose collection of texts – which had been periodically augmented, redacted, and amended over a period of 250 years – and became a stable text, a physical book capable of being reproduced and studied on a mass scale.[23] Given these historical factors, the stage was set for Kabbalistic ideas and practices to expand, evolve, infiltrate, and eventually assume centre stage within Jewish homes, study halls, texts, customs, legal coda, and liturgy.

Kabbalah's expansion and infiltration did not go unnoticed. During the early modern period, in which Kabbalah conquered much of the Jewish world, a small yet powerful cadre of scholars raised their voices against these novel strains of theological imagination. Three voices in particular stand out as the principal representatives of the anti-Kabbalistic (or more specifically, anti-Zoharic) tradition within Jewish thought. These three scholars alone produced works of significant length and rabbinic erudition to truly mount

---

[23] For an exhaustive account of the Zohar's journey from manuscript to book, see: Daniel Abrams, "The Invention of the Zohar as a Book", *Kabbalah*, Vol. 19 (2009) pp. 7-142.

an effective broadside against the legitimacy of the Kabbalah and the authenticity of the Zohar.[24]

The first such work was *Behinat Ha-dat* (Crete, 1491), authored by the Italian rationalist philosopher Elijah del Medigo (1458-1493).[25] One of the last great defenders of Aristotelian philosophy within Jewish thought, del Medigo's work may be categorised as essentially a rearguard action of the thoroughly beleaguered Maimonidean school, which attempted to demonstrate the superiority of interpretations of Judaism that conformed to fashionable strains of medieval philosophy.[26] In his eyes, the discipline of philosophy was

---

[24] For a more extensive history of Zohar criticism, see: Boaz Huss, *The Zohar: Reception and Impact*, Transl. Judith Nave (Liverpool University Press, 2016) pp. 239-294. This history is also documented in Tishby's lengthy introduction to his monumental *Mishnat Ha-Zohar*, vol. 1 (Mossad Bialik, 1949) pp. 17-116. This introduction is also available in the English translation: Isaiah Tishby, *The Wisdom of the Zohar: An Anthology of Texts*, Transl. David Goldstein (Liverpool University Press, 1989) pp. 1-126.

[25] Interestingly, there are some seemingly contradictory statements regarding Jewish mysticism throughout del Medigo's oeuvre, leading to the possibility that his views evolved during his life due to new knowledge or ideological shifts. See: Kalman Bland, "Elijah del Medigo's Averroist Response to the Kabbalahs of Fifteenth-Century Jewry and Pico della Mirandola", *The Journal of Jewish Thought and Philosophy*, Vol. 1, no. 1 (1991) pp. 23-53.

[26] The interactions between philosophy and religion within del Medigo's work were complex and shifting, as outlined by David Geffen in: *Faith and Reason in Elijah del Medigo's 'Behinat ha-dat' and*

crucial for purifying Judaic doctrines and clarifying the meanings of its holy texts, and therefore all forms of irrationalism constitute a threat to its continuity. It was this fervent faith in the centrality of rationalism that fuelled del Medigo's historical and ideological barrage (the first extended one of its kind) against the Zohar.

On the historical plane, del Medigo noted the grave unlikelihood of such a prominent text remaining a perfectly guarded secret for over a millennium. Surely, he maintained, if the Zohar was indeed a Mishnaic-era text, then it would have commanded great authority among the Talmudic, Geonic, and medieval authorities, who would have based their legal and philosophical pronouncements upon it. Yet, these central figures within the Jewish tradition all passed over the Zohar in uniform silence. Worse still, del Medigo pointed out that many of the Zohar's doctrines amounted to nothing less than a litany of theological heresies and philosophical errors. For del Medigo, the Zohar's depiction of divinity and creation in decidedly Neo-Platonic terms was a philosophical scandal, as this worldview had been conclusively eviscerated by the Neo-Aristotelian

---

the Philosophic Backgrounds of the Work (PhD Dissertation, Columbia University, 1970).

rationalists. Furthermore, the idea that human actions carried a theurgic power that could rectify or perfect the divine realm was not only doctrinally unsound but philosophically illiterate. Human beings, even with all the religious rituals ever devised, could not possibly presume to come to the aid of a perfect Being. Del Medigo's assault, therefore, was multi-pronged. He both lambasted Kabbalah as a relatively recent invention with mere pretensions towards canonicity, and also pointed out the dangers inherent in substituting a rationally sound form of Judaism with an outdated, occultic theology.

Although initially written at the end of the fifteenth century, *Behinat Ha-dat* was only printed in 1629, along with a rebuttal by the author's descendant Joseph Solomon del Medigo (or *Yasha"r Mi-Candia*, 1591-1665).[27] Yet, until it was republished in 1833 by

---

[27] *Yasha"r Mi-Candia* published a two-part anthology entitled *Ta'alumot Hokhmah* (Basel, 1629-1631), which included a section called *Mazref La-Hokhmah*, in which he both reproduces, and attempts to refute the claims of, his ancestor's anti-Kabbalistic polemic, *Behinat Ha-dat*. The question of Yashar's own true opinions regarding Kabbalah, and whether his protests in *Mazref La-Hokhmah* were merely an elaborate ruse to maintain good standing among traditionalists, is the subject of recent scholarly speculation. This is especially so since the publication of an anthology titled *Melo Hofnayim* edited by Abraham Geiger in 1840,

the Maskilic author Isaac Samuel Reggio (or *Yasha"r Mi-Gorizia*, 1784-1855), this work of Kabbalah criticism failed to make a significant impact in the wider rabbinic world.

That honour was reserved for Judah Aryeh (or Leon) of Modena (1571-1648), perhaps the most brilliant and unconventional rabbinic leaders of Italian Jewry during the Early Modern period. Modena lived during a period in which Kabbalah was enjoying a brief yet impressive vogue among learned Christian Humanists such Giovanni Pico della Mirandola (1463-1494) and Johannes Reuchlin (1455-1522), both of whom placed Kabbalah at the centre of their own ecumenical Christian theologies. Modena also witnessed the ineluctable spread of Kabbalah throughout his own Jewish community, largely due to the indefatigable evangelisers of Lurianic Kabbalah such as Ḥayyim Vital (1543-1620). Modena watched with increasing consternation as many of his rabbinic colleagues, close disciples, and even members of his own family

in which he reproduces what he claims to be an anti-Kabbalistic tract authored by *Yasha"r Mi-Candia*, thus complicating the latter's legacy. On this, see: David B. Ruderman, *Jewish Thought and Scientific Discovery in Early Modern Europe* (Yale University Press, 1995), p. 118-152.

assimilated Kabbalah into their own Jewish learning and praxis. This combination of Christian encroachment, combined with the replacement of Maimonidean-style rationalism with Zoharic and Lurianic mysticism, drove Modena to write a book-length attack on Kabbalah, which he titled *Ari Nohem* (Venice, 1639).[28]

While Modena regurgitates several of the philosophical charges laid at the door of Kabbalah, the bulk of his work is dedicated to undermining the Zohar's claims to antiquity and authenticity. After reproducing Isaac of Acre's testimony from the *Sefer Yuḥasin* concerning de Leon's authorship of the Zohar, Modena follows Azariah dei Rossi (1511-1578) in expanding the litany of anachronisms evident throughout the length and breadth of the Zohar. Such historical difficulties included the following points:

---

[28] The precise motivations for Modena's work remain a matter of dispute. Yaacob Dweck has argued that Modena's reasoning was largely internal, a result of Modena's opposition to the ideas and practices of his contemporaries. See: Yaacob Dweck, *The Scandal of Kabbalah: Leon Modena, Jewish Mysticism, Early Modern Venice* (Princeton University Press, 2011) pp. 61-100. Moshe Idel, by contrast, has made the case that Modena's primary goal was combatting the pernicious encroachment of Christian Kabbalah. See: Moshe Idel, "Differing Conceptions of Kabbalah in the Early Seventeenth Century", in: *Jewish Thought in the Seventeenth Century*, B. Septimus, I. Twersky, eds, (Harvard University Press, 1979) pp. 137-200.

- Many important figures quoted or invoked in the Zohar lived several generations after the second century CE, and therefore could not have been known to Rabbi Shimon bar Yoḥai and his immediate circle.

- The complete absence of the Zohar in the history of Jewish legal discourse, as well as the quite blatant contradictions between the legal pronouncements of the Zohar and the accepted Halakha in the Talmud and medieval texts.

- Several historical events described in the Zohar, including the rise of Islam and the advent of the Crusades, took place several centuries after the Zohar's purported composition.

- Similarly, several liturgical compositions are referred to in the Zohar that were only composed during the Geonic period, at the very earliest.

- The Zohar was written largely in Judeo-Aramaic. Seeing as Aramaic was the spoken lingua franca among ordinary Jews in ancient Judea, it would have made little sense to compose a mystical tract in this language rather than rabbinic Hebrew, which was in fact the language of the scholarly elite. Conversely, in medieval Spain, where rabbinic scholars spent much of their time wading through the complex Judeo-Aramaic dialect in the Babylonian Talmud, writing the Zohar in Aramaic would have been an effective gatekeeping strategy.

- The use of certain words that stem from medieval romance languages, (including the famous pun in which the synagogue – Esnoga in medieval Spanish – is described as an '*esh noga*', or 'burning fire'), which demonstrate the Zohar's composition in Western Europe.

Despite this quite formidable list of accusation, Modena remained at least somewhat enamoured by the Zohar as a literary artefact, expressing admiration for its exquisite wordsmithery and hermeneutical ingenuity. In other words, despite being a staunch opponent of Kabbalah itself, he was quite clearly charmed by its major texts, and thus retained a general tone of respect and sympathy throughout.

The third great early modern critic of the Zohar, the rabbinic titan Jacob Emden (1697-1776), appeared entirely impervious to the charms of the Zohar. As is evidenced by his other works, Emden's quite remarkable range of competence included the texts and ideas of Kabbalah, which he utilised freely throughout much of his oeuvre.[29] Yet it was the flagrant misuse of Kabbalah by supporters of the Sabbatean movement, and especially his incorrigible *bête noire* Rabbi Jonathan Eibeschütz, that sparked Emden's ire. Emden thus adopted an intricate, even paradoxical approach towards Kabbalah, venerating its true teachings while denouncing its fraudulent and antinomian elements that had taken root within significant segments of European Jewry. It is precisely this tension that characterises Emden's *Mitpaḥat Sefarim* (Altona, 1768). This extraordinary work is at once a full-throated defence of, and vituperative attack against, the Kabbalistic tradition. After a pious throat-clearing, in which Emden defends the authentic, holy, and pristine core of true Jewish mysticism, he trains his razor-sharp critical scalpel on the Zoharic corpus. The result is the most systematic, thorough, and excoriating

---

[29]Emden himself wrote a dictionary of Kabbalah (*Tzitzim U-Ferachim*, Altona, 1768), and his commentary on the Jewish prayer book also included mystical themes. For a consideration of Emden's complex and apparently self-contradictory views on Kabbalah, see: Tamara Morsel-Eisenberg, "Mysticism, Rationalism, and Criticism: Rabbi Jacob Emden as an Early Modern Critic and Printer", *Harvard Theological Review* Vol. 115, no. 1 (2022) pp. 110–35; Moshe Idel, "Perceptions of Kabbalah in the Second Half of the 18th Century", *The Journal of Jewish Thought and Philosophy* Vol. 1, no. 1 (1992) pp. 55–114.

demolition of the Zohar in the long history of rabbinic writing.

In truth, much of the *Mitpaḥat Sefarim* simply sharpens, amplifies, and deepens the criticisms outlined by del Medigo, Modena, and others. However, Emden's sharp eyes and encyclopaedic knowledge of the entire gamut of Jewish texts enabled him to point out a quite startling list of errors that run the length and breadth of the Zohar, including:

- Misattributed or erroneous statements placed into the mouths of Talmudic rabbis.
- Legal decisions that contravene the accepted Halakha as stated in the Talmud.
- Biographical and genealogical assertions that blatantly contradict the information found in the Talmud.
- Errors of geography and topography, strongly indicating that the authors of the Zoharic texts had never visited the Land of Israel.
- Preposterous or unacceptable readings of biblical verses.
- The extravagant glorification of Rabbi Shimon bar Yoḥai, which occasionally strays into the realm of deification.

Most consequentially, however, was Emden's foray into the history of the Bible's vowels and cantillation notes (*Nequdot* and *Te'amim*), which constitute the bulk of the Masoretic apparatus present in all extant copies of the Hebrew Bible. Statements within the Rabbinic corpus[30] claims this system of vocalisation to be very ancient indeed, originating either with the original writing of the biblical texts or else instituted by Ezra upon the instauration of the Jerusalem temple in the fifth century BCE. However, by Emden's era, both Jewish and Christian opinion on this subject had progressed.[31] Elijah Levita (*Eliyahu Baḥur*, 1469-1549) one of the premier grammarians and Hebraists of the early modern period, had constructed a powerful case for dating the *Nequdot* and *Te'amim* to the work of the Tiberian Masoretes, no earlier than the fifth century CE. Emden endorses and extends Levita's conclusions, noting that the numerous Zoharic passages that specify and even glorify the vowels of the Hebrew language could not possibly have been written during the Mishnaic period. This point,

---

[30] See, for instance, *Megillah* 3a; *Nedarim* 37b.
[31] For an overview of this history, see: Jordan S. Penkower, "S.D. Luzzatto, Vowels and Accents, and the Date of the Zohar", in: *Samuel David Luzzatto: The Bi-Centennial of his Birth* [Hebrew], R. Bonfils, I. Gottlieb, H. Kasher, Eds. (Magnes Press, 2004) pp. 79-130, p. 125-129.

elaborated upon by later scholars, would prove to be a linchpin of the case for the late dating of the Zohar.

All told, Emden marshalled close to 300 examples demonstrating the lateness of the Zohar and the patent fraudulence of many of its sections. So thorough and multi-faceted was Emden's work that it served as the substantial basis for all future Zohar criticism, leading some intellectuals of the Haskalah movement to claim Emden as an important precursor to their own critical investigations into prior Jewish texts.[32] Yet, as an unimpeachably Orthodox rabbinic figure and Kabbalist himself, Emden sought to chart a delicate middle course between traditionalism and critical scholarship. He drew a distinction between an authentic 'core' of the Zohar which he believed stretched back to the Talmudic period, and the many later accretions and interpolations (including whole sections of the Zohar such as the *Ra'aya Mehemna, Tiqqune Zohar,* and the *Ma'amare Ha-Piqqudin*) which he viewed as patently fabricated and fallacious. Thus, despite extensively mapping the Zohar's

---

[32]The question of whether Emden may be seen as a bridge between traditional and Maskilic modes of Jewish scholarship is a subject of historiographic debate and has been adjudicated by Shmuel Feiner in his work *The Jewish Enlightenment*, transl. Chaya Naor (University of Pennsylvania Press, 2002) p. 30-35.

various legal, historical, geographical, philological, and theological incongruities, Emden's general approach nonetheless leaves sufficient space for the devout Jew to preserve their religious veneration of Kabbalah, albeit a far leaner version of its texts and doctrines.[33] Emden's arguments and attitudes were influential among his rabbinic colleagues, and have been subsequently endorsed by numerous authorities, including most notably Moses Sofer (*Ḥatam Sofer*, 1762-1839).[34]

---

[33] This general attitude of distancing from Kabbalah without disavowing it altogether has been a fairly common practice among certain Jewish communities of the modern era. Among Ashkenazim, this includes the nineteenth century Neo-Orthodox communities in Western Europe. Among Sepharadim, this includes the Yemenites and the Spanish & Portuguese Jewish communities. Although Rabbi Yosef Ḥayyim's nineteenth century *Ben Ish Ḥai* spearheaded much of the Kabbalistic influence on Sepharadi *halakha*, Rabbi Obadya Yosef succeeded in limiting this influence within his own legal deliberations.

[34] Sofer's statement on this issue is laconic and opaque, yet nonetheless speaks volumes as to his acknowledgement of support for Emden's position regarding the Zohar and Kabbalah. In his *Responsa of the Ḥatam Sofer*, Volume 6, subsection 59, he writes the following.

הנה נמצא בשכונתך ס' מטפחת ספרים למהריעב"ץ תמצא שם
כי דבר גדול דבר הנביא בענין זה הלא ישתוממו רואיו וד"ל.

[Translation: You may find in your area the book Mitpaḥat Sefarim by our master, Rabbi Ya'aqob Emden. You will find there a great thing that this prophet [i.e., Emden] has spoken regarding this matter, and it will surely astonish those who see it. And this is sufficient for the wise.]

The rise of the European Haskalah from the 1770s onwards heralded a new age of scholarship and attitudes concerning Kabbalah. The first generation of Maskilim, including major Jewish *Aufklärer* such as Moses Mendelssohn (1729-1786) and Naphtali Hirz Wessely (1725-1805), recognised Kabbalah as antithetical to their collective project of an enlightened Judaism. Yet, like Emden,[35] they preferred to minimise its presence in their modern configurations of Judaism, without undercutting its legitimacy outright. Mendelssohn even went so far as to utilise the Zohar when the occasion called for it, as for instance in the introduction to his commentary on Ecclesiastes (Berlin, 1769), where he invoked the Zohar to demonstrate the centrality of the doctrine of the immortality of the soul. Within this Mendelssohnian school of enlightened domestication of Kabbalah stood other Maskilim such as Salomon Maimon (1753-1800), Isaac Satanow (1732-1804), and Nachman Krochmal (1785-1840), all of whom posited the existence of a pure, vital, and authoritative core of Kabbalistic mysticism, which had

---

[35] Mendelssohn praised Emden's *Mitpaḥat Sefarim* in the introduction to his Commentary to the Pentateuch (*Or La-Netivah*, Vienna 1846, p. xvi), stating that it had provided incontrovertible proof against the antiquity of the Zohar.

sadly degenerated due to the vicissitudes of Jewish history.[36]

Yet, with the onset of the nineteenth century and the rise of a second, more radical generation of Maskilim, this cautious respect for Kabbalah gave way to unveiled scorn and antipathy. These decades also witnessed the epicentre of the three-way pitched battle between three major ideological camps – Ḥasidim, Mitnaggedim, and Maskilim – each accusing the other of subverting or misguiding the true Jewish faith in favour of their own newfangled credos. One casualty of this war was Kabbalah, which found itself under unflagging attack from a bevy of Maskilic authors, whose weapon of choice was parody and satire.[37] In this context, a wide array of plays, pamphlets, and spoof scholarship

---

[36] For a discussion of these thinkers and their Kabbalistic systems, see: Horowitz, *Kabbalah*; David Biale, "The Kabbalah in Nachman Krochmal's Philosophy of History", *Journal of Jewish Studies*, Vol. 32 (1981), pp. 85-97; Gideon Freudenthal, "Salomon Maimon's Development from Kabbalah to Philosophical Rationalism." *Tarbiz*, Vol. 80, no. 1 (2012), pp. 105-171; Uri Gershowitz, "Kabbalah and Philosophy in the Early Works of Salomon Maimon." *RUDN Journal of Philosophy*, Vol. 24, no. 3 (2020), pp. 342–61.

[37] A fuller treatment of this subject was produced by Yehudah Friedlander in his two books: *Hebrew Satire and Polemics in Europe During the 18-20th Centuries* [Hebrew] (Bar Ilan University Press, 2004) pp.17-178; *Studies in Hebrew Satire in Germany 1790-1797* [Hebrew] (Tel Aviv University Press, 1989).

lampooning Hasidism and Kabbalah came to the fore. In the Germanic states, the writings of figures such as Saul Levine-Berlin (1740-1794) and Aaron Wolfson (1754-1835) attacked the Jewish mystical tradition as false and superstitious, while those at the front lines of this ideological war in Poland and Galicia, such as Menachem Mendel Lefin (1749-1826), Tobias Feder (1760–1817), and Isaac Baer Levisohn (1788-1860), expanded on this satirical tradition by attacking the aesthetic, theological, and even ethical qualities of the Zoharic texts. One motif was consistent within these satirical works: that Jewish communities could only assume their full moral and intellectual height when standing over the tomb of medieval mysticism and associated superstitions. Perhaps the most brutal of these parodies was Judah Loeb Mises' *Kinat Ha'emet* (Vienna, 1828), which depicts a celestial conversation between the souls of Maimonides and a well-known Kabbalistic author by the name of Solomon Helmah of Chelm. Using both these figures as mouthpieces, Mises fulminates against the Zohar as a work of irredeemable fraudulence and worthlessness, responsible for poisoning the pristine Judaic religion with all manner of superstitious nonsense.

While such works certainly broadened the genre of Zohar criticism, they provided little depth. For all their literary verve and erudite humour, Maskilim of the late eighteenth and early nineteenth centuries failed to produce treatises exploring the issues surrounding the Zohar and Kabbalah with appropriate depth and rigour. It was left to the scholars of the nineteenth century – especially those associated with the *Wissenschaft des Judentums* movement, whose investigations into Jewish history and culture laid the basis for Jewish studies to this day – to continue the tradition of Kabbalah criticism within more ideologically sober and methodologically rigorous parameters.

It is at this point in the history of Kabbalah scholarship that the two sets of epistolary exchanges, as translated and published in this present volume, come to hand.

3: Letters between Shadal and Rabbi Benamozegh

The first set of letters presented in this volume stem from the pens of a pair of truly remarkable nineteenth century intellectuals: Samuel David Luzzatto (Shadal, 1800-1865) and Elijah Benamozegh (1823-1900).

There were few men in Jewish history quite like Shadal. Dazzlingly erudite, voluminously productive, and almost implausibly diverse in his expertise, Shadal – who was described by one prominent historian as "the greatest Jew in an age so peculiarly rich with great Jews" – was a scholar almost without peer in his own century. Despite having a biography that reads like the book of Job, Shadal's remarkable mind and tireless pen produced dozens of books, hundreds of articles, and thousands of letters, disseminating his eclectic ideas in Hebrew, Italian, French, and German. His works broach the full range of Jewish subjects, including studies of Hebrew and Aramaic philology; analyses of medieval and modern poetry; translations and commentaries of many books of the Hebrew Bible; a new Italian edition of the siddur; original Hebrew poems; a massive variety of introductory essays, historical monographs, and biographical profiles; as well as a cache of erudite personal correspondence, the published version of which fills nine volumes.

For the purposes of this volume, Shadal's most relevant work was his *Vikuaḥ Al Ḥokhmat Ha-Kabbalah, Ve-al Qadmut Sefer Ha-Zohar, Ve-Qadmut Ha-Nequdot Ve-ha-Te'amim*, or "Dialogue Concerning the Wisdom of the Kabbalah, The Antiquity of the Zohar, and the Antiquity of the Vowelisation and Cantillation Marks"

(Gorizia, 1852).[38] This literary-philosophical dialogue was penned when Shadal was only 26 years old, and reflects Shadal's very early preoccupation with, and antipathy towards, Kabbalah.[39] Its storyline depicts two fictional scholars – the 'Author' and the 'Guest' – debating the antiquity and legitimacy of Judaism's mystical traditions. While the constraints of space in this introduction do not permit anything like a full analysis of Shadal's *Dialogue*,[40] three brief observations do warrant our focus. First, unlike almost all other Jewish dialogues (Yehudah Halevi's *Kuzari* serving as the classic

---

[38] This work was subsequently published in a later collection of Shadal's essays, titled *Studies in Judaism* [Hebrew] (Warsaw, 1913), pp.113-240. This work was recently republished in 2013 (Ed. Jonathan Bassi, Carmel Press). I have recently finished an academic translation of this work, which is slated to be released in 2024 by Palgrave Macmillan.

[39] This aversion to Kabbalah was so strong that the thirteen-year-old Shadal – to the outrage of his desperate father – refused to utter mystical prayers on behalf of his own dying mother, giving the reason that these prayers were of Kabbalistic origin and therefore theologically illegitimate. This heart-wrenching story, as well as the progression of his antipathy towards Kabbalah, is relayed by Shadal himself in: Samuel David Luzzatto, *Chapters of my life* [Hebrew], Ed. M. Schulwas (New York, 1951), p. 17-22.

[40] For a full analysis of this truly extraordinary work, readers will have to wait for my forthcoming translation of Shadal's *Dialogue* (projected publication 2024, Palgrave Macmillan), in which I provide a lengthy introduction discussing this work's literary, historical, and philosophical elements.

exemplar), it constitutes a genuine debate between a pair of well-matched opponents. Shadal's two antagonists are both depicted as immensely literate, fully capable of harnessing a wide array of logical and textual proofs in support of their position. Second, Shadal's *Dialogue* is a finely crafted literary gem, in which plot, tempo, setting, humour, rhetorical strategy, as well as the lyrical Maskilic Hebrew all contribute to its pedagogical force. Third, Shadal's *Dialogue* is more wide-ranging and sophisticated than any previous work of Zohar criticism, drawing as it does upon elements of Jewish history, philosophy, philology, liturgy, theology, literature, and law throughout its deliberations. It is therefore little wonder that Shadal's immensely readable and intellectually omnivorous dialogue was perceived by many as the most wounding attack on the Kabbalah and its central texts ever penned by a significant rabbinic scholar.

Conceived as such, it was only natural that responses to Shadal's attacks would arise from among the Kabbalists. Of those who attempted to write a rebuttal, by far the most significant was Rabbi Elijah Benamozegh (1822-1900), another accomplished and controversial member of the Italian rabbinate. Benamozegh's powerfully paradoxical worldview, into which he interwove particularism and universalism, modernity and tradition, scientific research and mystical exuberance, has recently (and justifiably) become a subject of scholarly attention.[41] It was Benamozegh, a prominent adherent and defender of Kabbalah, who composed the lengthiest and most sustained rebuttal to Shadal's *Dialogue*.[42] Despite his best efforts, however, Benamozegh's work (much like the rest of his oeuvre) fails to reach the rigour, sophistication, or literary sparkle of his more senior rabbinic colleague.

Receiving no public response to his rebuttal, Benamozegh took up his pen and began a contentious exchange of letters with Shadal, the edited version of which takes up the first part of this present volume.[43]

---

[41] Benamozegh's idiosyncratic worldview has been best explored by Clemence Boulouque, in her work *Another Modernity: Eliyahu Benamozegh's Jewish Universalism* (Stanford University Press, 2020). Another useful work on the subject is Alessandro Guetta's *Philosophy and Kabbalah: Elijah Benamozegh and the Reconciliation of Western Thought and Jewish Esotericism* (State University of New York Press, 2009).

[42] *Ta'am LaShad*, (Livorno, 1863).

[43] I encourage readers to peruse Daniel A. Klein's introduction and contextualisation of these letters, in which he lays out in far more detail the process and results of this exchange. See: Daniel A. Klein, "Let Him Bray: The Stormy Correspondence Between Samuel David Luzzatto and Eliyahu Benamozegh", *Hakirah*, Vol. 31 (2021) pp. 269–300.

Benamozegh expresses his disappointment that Shadal did not deign to respond to his book-length rebuttal, and expressed his outrage upon hearing that, in a letter to another colleague concerning Benamozegh's work, Shadal dismissively sniped "let him bray". This casual insult precipitated their epistolary exchange between the months of August 1863 and March 1864. Benamozegh's letters exhibit an almost cringeworthy desire to be considered by Shadal as an equal, a friend, and a worthy intellectual adversary. His letters are therefore a maelstrom of intermingled admiration, confusion, and umbrage. He alternates between shameless flattery, declarations of loyalty, substantive criticism, and pained invective, all deployed in an attempt to coax Shadal into engaging with him both intellectually and personally.

Sadly, Benamozegh was howling into the void. By 1863, Shadal was nearing the end of his earthly sojourn, and he knew it. Blind, bereaved of five of his children, chronically ill, and thoroughly exhausted by decades of grinding poverty, Shadal was in no shape to engage in this intricate and highly volatile debate. Short on life, Shadal was also short on patience. He repeatedly rebuffs his younger colleague's attempt to engage him on the subject at hand, as well as his overtures for friendship and parity. Such letters make for difficult reading, especially for those familiar with the open-minded camaraderie and polymathic brilliance of Shadal's better years, during which his incisive pen was at once loved and feared by Jewish intelligentsia across Europe. This asymmetrical exchange of letters, as fascinating and thought-provoking as they are, leave the reader with a sense of sadness at their unfortunate timing. Had Benamozegh, the apologist par excellence for Kabbalah, been able to engage productively with Shadal during his incandescent prime, who knows what intellectual treasures may have been generated? Tragically, this will forever remain a counterfactual.

4: Letters between Rabbi Kook and Rabbi Qafiḥ

The second set of letters in this volume feature an exchange between the two towering rabbinic figures of the early twentieth century: Yiḥye Qafiḥ (1850-1932) and Abraham Isaac Kook (1865-1935).[44]

Rabbi Qafiḥ's ultimately doomed attempt to promulgate a quasi-Haskalah in his native Yemen is a truly fascinating episode in Jewish cultural history. One of the great Halakhists and community leaders of his day, Rabbi Qafiḥ noted with dismay that Yemenite Jewry had not only failed to follow their once-regnant

---

[44] Originally found in *Shevut Teiman* (1945), 166–231.

Maimonidean tradition, but had replaced it with all manner of mysticism and local superstition. Study of the Zohar had displaced the study of more traditional exoteric texts, while the use of amulets, charms, pseudo-medicines, and other magical paraphernalia had become the norm. With admirable courage and self-confidence, Rabbi Qafiḥ sought to re-orient his native community away from mysticism and back towards non-Kabbalistic forms of Talmudic and Halakhic Judaism.

His attempted reforms were both social and educational. Even as he sought a restoration of old Yemenite customs, he also worked towards an educational revolution within the *Yeshibot* and *Batte Midrash* under his influence. Gone was the Zohar and other mystical *Midrashim*, while the works of the great Judeo-Arabic philosophers such as Se'adya Gaon, Baḥya Ibn Paquda, and Maimonides were enshrined at the centre of his new curriculum. Rabbi Qafiḥ gathered around him a cadre of scholars and disciples who became known as the *Darda'im* (an Arabic contraction of the Hebrew *Dor De'ah*, or 'generation of knowledge'), and for a short period at the peak of his powers it seemed that the Yemenite community could become an unlikely hub of enlightened Jewish thought and practice.

Yet Rabbi Qafiḥ and his movement encountered stiff resistance from their very inception. This was largely due to his uncompromising crusade against Kabbalah and its attendant folkloric practices, which he dismissed as not only foreign to the Jewish tradition, but its antithesis. His thunderous denunciations of the Zohar ensured his notoriety both in Yemen and around the Jewish world. He was denounced numerous times as a heretic by his rabbinic colleagues in Yemen and Jerusalem,[45] and was even incarcerated by the Muslim authorities in 1914 for his troubles. Yet such opposition only spurred Rabbi Qafiḥ's indomitable conviction in his own rationalist position. From the very same year of his incarceration, he began working on his major publication, *Milḥamoth HaShem* (Jerusalem, 1930-31), in which he reiterated an uncompromising form of the same arguments posited by predecessors such as Emden and Shadal: that the Zohar was a medieval forgery and that the Kabbalistic portrayal of the divine *Sefirot* constitute an idolatrous heresy.

---

[45] Some of this controversy and its ramifications has been covered by Marc B. Shapiro, in his Hebrew article: "Is there an obligation to believe that Rebbe Shimon bar Yochai wrote the Zohar?", *Milin Havivin*, Vol. 5 (2010-2011) Hebrew section, pp. 1-20.

It was to various claims of this kind that Rabbi Abraham Isaac Kook, the Chief Rabbi of Mandate Palestine at the time, addressed himself. 'Rav Kook', as he has come to be called, was a thinker whose breadth and complexity defies conventional categorisation. Like many of the most fruitful thinkers, his intellectual influences were broad and varied.[46] His transcendence of traditional boundaries, both in his ideology and personal comportment, rendered him wildly popular in some circles and thoroughly reviled in others. His strong attraction to Kabbalah made him an outlier in the strictly Lithuanian-style atmosphere of the Volozhin Yeshiva; his support for the Zionist project rendered him unpalatable to most of his Orthodox rabbinic contemporaries; and his irrepressibly religious strivings painted him as a quaint curiosity within pre-state Israel's politics and society. Yet Rav Kook spent his entire life attempting to transcend what he viewed as illusory divisions. He never tired of emphasising the essential,

---

[46] For the intellectual development of Rav Kook, the English reader can do no better than to read Yehuda Mirsky's two splendid books on the subject: *Rav Kook: Mystic in a time of revolution* (Yale University Press, 2014); *Towards the Mystical Experience of Modernity: The Making of Rav Kook, 1865-1904* (Academic Studies Press, 2021).

underlying unity from which all entities stemmed, as well as the ultimate coalescence that all of creation would achieve in the messianic age, in which all apparent division, strife, and incompatibility would be overcome. In short, Rav Kook's Edenic vision for Jewry and for all mankind was rooted in a thoroughly Kabbalistic understanding of creation, revelation, and redemption. It is little wonder, therefore, that Rav Kook – generally a peacemaker among his rabbinic colleagues – reacted with some alarm to the news coming from Yemen of an anti-Kabbalistic revolution.

This sets the stage for brief exchange of rabbinic letters that are to be found in the second half of this volume. These two letters, written in 1931 towards the end of both men's lives, are quite unlike the Shadal-Benamozegh exchange in that they adhere strictly to the literary and religious conventions of rabbinic epistles. They are formal, pious, self-effacing, obsequious (at least most of the time), rhetorically pugnacious, and suffused with references to the canonical texts of the Jewish tradition.

Yet these letters are a luminous window not only into the opinions of the two authors on the merits of Kabbalah – which themselves stand worthy of consideration – but also to their sharply divergent personalities. Rav Kook's letter is typically genial, inclusive, and conciliatory, and appears to be labouring under the (self-inflicted?) delusion that his Yemenite counterpart has simply been a victim of some kind of intellectual mishap. Surely, his benign letter seems to imply, once Rabbi Qafiḥ has been apprised of this new information, he will join the rest of the Orthodox rabbinate in their high opinion of Kabbalah. Yet Rabbi Qafiḥ remained utterly resolute. His response resembles little less than a barrage of proofs, questions, and fulminations that reflect not only the remarkable range of his scholarship but also his frustration that so many of his rabbinic colleagues appear to have been taken in by Kabbalah, which in his eyes blatantly contradict the Talmudic and Halakhic Judaism which he felt duty-bound to defend. He refuses to budge an inch on the topic of Kabbalah, and Rav Kook appears to have taken the wise decision not to press his case any further.

Finally, it is worth noting that Rabbi Qafiḥ includes the signatures of four other Yemenite rabbis at the bottom of his letter, clearly indicating that he is buttressed not only by his formidable scholarship but also by the consensus of those authorities belonging to his school of thought. This list of signatures, it would seem, was intended to send a clear message to Rabbi Kook, as well as his less convivial colleagues who wished for nothing more than Qafiḥ's silent acquiescence: *I will not be intimidated.*

5: Conclusion

In short, the two sets of letters presented in this volume are important primary documents that belong to the intellectual tradition outlined above, namely the 700-year debate regarding the antiquity, authenticity, and legitimacy of Kabbalah. That they have now been brought within the reach of an English-speaking audience is a source of pride and gratitude.

My profound obeisances go to the translators of these exchanges. Daniel A. Klein, the premier Shadal translator of our day, has done a typically splendid job of bringing the florid Italian prose to life, rendering the imperishable writings of these two giants not only comprehensible but immensely enjoyable.[47] Ben Rothstein's task was perhaps even more daunting. Translating the enigmatic and endlessly referential rabbinic Hebrew in such a way that both highlights and

---

[47] Daniel A. Klein's translation originally appeared in: Daniel A. Klein, "Let Him Bray: The Stormy Correspondence Between Samuel David Luzzatto and Eliyahu Benamozegh", *Hakirah*, Vol. 31 (2021) pp. 269-300. The translation also appears as Appendix B to Klein's edition of *Shadal on Numbers* (Kodesh Press, 2023).

lightens the intellectual load is no mean feat, and he has achieved this with considerable proficiency. Both of these gentlemen may take pride in the fact that their work shall, for years to come, facilitate the consideration and discussion of a range of nettlesome yet intriguing issues within contemporary Judaic discourse.

Finally, the leaders of The Ḥabura and Da'at Press, who have conceived of this important book and shepherded it to its final publication, are to be commended for taking bold steps in the dissemination of knowledge and illumination.

כן ירבה וכן יפרוץ.

J.J. Kimche
Bala Cynwyd, Pennsylvania, USA
July 2023 / Tammuz 5783

Letters Between

Rabbi Eliyahu Benamozegh

&

Shadal

Translated by Daniel A. Klein

Translator's Note

The Benamozegh-Shadal correspondence reproduced here was sparked by a minor incident that occurred in 1863. In "Le Missioni di Terra Santa," a pamphlet that offered support for charitable emissaries from the land of Israel, Benamozegh sardonically remarked in passing that "Professor Luzzatto" had expressed certain views that were "more Orthodox than the Masters of Orthodoxy." Shadal decided not to respond, but in a private letter to a third party, he confided, "I intend to let him bray." Somehow this comment came to Benamozegh's attention, and he wrote Shadal to express his displeasure.

From there, the correspondence branched off into a testy exchange of views on the Kabbalah and assorted other matters. After replying at length to three of Benamozegh's letters, Shadal apparently grew tired of the exchange and left three more of his rival's letters unanswered. Benamozegh's side of the correspondence was printed in *Lettere Dirette a S. D. Luzzatto da Elia Benamozegh* (Livorno, 1890), while Shadal's responses were included in a separate collection of his letters, the multilingual *Epistolario Italiano Francese Latino* (Padua, 1890).

All of the letters in their exchange were written in the high literary style of their century, laced with flashes of wit and sarcasm. In translating the letters from their flowery, almost operatic Italian, I added explanatory footnotes to flesh out the often fascinating backgrounds to some of their more obscure references. One of the editors of this volume has contributed an additional footnote of their own.

None of the nine letters in this collection is presented here in its entirety. Each one has been edited to omit some extraneous matter and to focus on the most essential arguments (note that Benamozegh's full letter of Sept. 21, 1863, alone runs to 30 printed pages). What remains, however, is more than enough to shed remarkable light on the writers' principles and personalities, and on their treatment of key issues that remain relevant to Jewish thought today.

Daniel A. Klein

Letter 1

Rabbi Benamozegh to Shadal

Date: August 16, 1863

Most esteemed Sir and friend,

...I want to give you now a proof of the great account in which I hold your opinion, and at the same time the honesty of my conduct. It would displease me greatly— disposed as each of us are, I have no doubt, to love and respect the adversary as a man of honour and a friend— if misunderstandings arose that could poison the relations between us that I always wish to keep cordial. Through information that I have reason to believe beyond any suspicion, I know for certain... that you, having had occasion to express yourself in writing concerning my polemic, availed yourself of this precise phrase: *lasciatelo ragliare* ("let him bray").

Samuel D. Luzzatto holds himself in such noble regard, he is so free of mean-spirited passions, he has such fame that none can obscure, that he could not possibly have used such indecencies, for which reason I could surely vouch that you are not their author. It is no less true, however, that they circulate in your name and perhaps have been put into the service of passions or schemes that are quite other than noble. This cannot and will not be. Your name cannot serve as an instrument of denigration, nor do I deserve to be repaid, against your will, with such coin for the respect that I have invariably shown and will show for you. I therefore believe that I have looked after your dignity by giving notice of this matter and submitting a demand upon your honesty for an explicit declaration that would paralyse the effects of a denigration that cloaks itself in your most reputable name....

I will leave off for today, requesting you to answer me and to keep in mind, when you wish to pay me some disagreeable compliment, to at least treat me as a *behemah tehorah* [a kosher animal].

Whether as a shade or as a real man, I will never cease to address myself to you as...

Most devoted and affectionate always,

Eliyahu Benamozegh

Letter 2

Shadal to Rabbi Benamozegh

Date: Aug. [no precise date given], 1863

Most esteemed friend,

I received some time ago the *Ta'am le-Shad*, and I did not write you so as not to enter into useless disputes. I was asked if I intended to respond, and I said no. And so it is. The little life and strength that are left to me[48] I wish to employ in endeavouring to leave to posterity a little more truth and a little less error, and not in fruitless

---

[48] Shadal was 63 and in failing health when he wrote this letter, and in fact he had only two more years to live. A few months previously, he had written to one of his students, "I am exhausted by old age and by melancholy.... Nevertheless, I persevere in my work. I do not wish to lose a solitary day, for who knows how few are the days left me? I must consolidate my work and get it published" (*Epistolario*, p. 1017, quoted in Margolies, *Samuel David Luzzatto*, p. 54).

controversies. Let anyone combat me who so desires; let anyone mistreat me at his pleasure; I will not waste my time in defending myself; I would be deflected from my mission, which is to discover new things. As long as there exists one verse in the Holy Scriptures that is not understood exactly, I must not think of defending my writings. Truth and time will defend them.

Besides, I cannot believe that you think you have refuted me. I do not believe that you are blinded. And if you believe it useful to defend mysticism, I will not oppose that.

Recently I saw your pamphlet about the Missionaries, and there I observed a page with libellous insinuations hurled needlessly against me, as if I were a hypocrite.[49] In this case I should have responded. But God made me strong, and I said and wrote in a confidential letter, *Penso lasciarlo ragliare*, never thinking that these words of mine could come to be used as weapons against you.[50] Nor did I intend to attribute to

---

[49] Evidently this is a reference to Benamozegh's comment, in "Le Missioni di Terra Santa," that those including Luzzatto who sought to dig an abyss between Greece and Palestine were "more Orthodox than the Masters of Orthodoxy."

[50] In fairness to Shadal, the phrase *Penso lasciarlo ragliare* ("I intend to let him bray"), worded as a private remark, is not the same as the phrase that Benamozegh accused him of using: *lasciatelo ragliare* ("let him bray," in the second person plural imperative, that is, as if Shadal were directly addressing the public at large).

you the nature of the braying quadruped, an animal that has always been held in higher esteem by me than is commonly the case.

"*S. D. L.,*" as you say in your letter, "*holds himself in a noble regard, is free of mean-spirited passions, and has such fame that none can obscure*"; therefore, upon seeing himself publicly treated as intolerant for lack of orthodoxy, he lets others bray.

The choice of word might have been less indecent if I had said *latrare* ("bark"). Crusca[51] would have offered me examples of barkers that are not dogs, but it gives me no example of brayers that are not donkeys. Still, braying seems to me less odious, less offensive than barking. In any case, you do not need me to declare to you that you have never been a donkey in my eyes; rather, I have used the verb *ragliare* by way of simile, just as Crusca has *latrare* as a simile.

And in so doing, it was not you who was the offended party, but the poor donkey. For the donkey's brayings are always sincere, that is, they are the

---

[51] This is a reference to the *Vocabolario degli Accademici della Crusca,* the first dictionary of the Italian language (first edition 1612). Shadal may have consulted the fourth edition (1729-1738). The publisher was the Accademia della Crusca, the world's oldest language academy, founded in Florence in 1583 and dedicated to separating the linguistic "wheat" from the corrupt *crusca,* or "bran."

expression of genuine feelings or sensations, such as hunger, love, or the like.

To the contrary, the words that were published by you against me in the aforementioned pamphlet express falsities and calumnies, not only against me, but equally against all the ancient masters who expressed an affinity for Greek culture, converting them all into so many apostates, similar to that Elisha [ben Abuyah] of whom it was said that "Greek tunes never ceased from his mouth" [Ḥagigah 15b]....

Live in happiness and believe me to be always a friend of the truth, and a friend of all men, but without hope or fear of them.

Your most devoted,
S. D. L.

Letter 3

Rabbi Benamozegh to Shadal

Date: Aug. 24, 1863 (Lettere, pp. 52-56)

Most esteemed friend,

If I were to act only out of self-love, I should not respond to your letter. Not only is the offence affirmed, but it is reaffirmed and pursued... But underneath your anger, which I believe to be undeserved, I still see the virtues and the selflessness that do you honour, and that is what makes me answer you. The fact that you prefer not to respond to the *Ta'am le-Shad*, not even privately... spares me the displeasure of finding myself once again in opposition to you. It is another thing, however, when you say, "Let anyone mistreat me who so desires." In my refutation, have I perhaps forgotten any of the requisite forms of respect? This I think you cannot say.

With regard to believing or not believing that I have refuted you, allow me to say to you that it is not up to me or you to judge, but with this difference: you may sincerely believe that I have not refuted you, while I could not, as you say, believe that I have not refuted you without being a charlatan or a writer in bad faith. I appeal to your good sense. Is it something to be envied nowadays, the defence of certain abandoned principles?

Is mystical theology so in vogue that one may be tempted to take up its defence, if a conviction that surpasses all other considerations did not obligate one to do so?... I make allowances for you because you do not know my life, my studies, my past; nor do you know how, after having loved the Kabbalistic books as a young man, I too began to speak ill of them seeing that everyone was doing so, and how it was only further reflections that brought me to believe that Mosaism without that theology was absolutely without basis... In sum, it would be inconceivable that I—having had such a wide scope for lashing out in the Kabbalistic polemic in *Ta'am le-Shad*— would have shown myself respectful in one whole volume but irreverent in four incidental words. That cannot be and is not the case.

Let us not speak of the minute disquisition concerning *latrare*, *ragliare*, etc...this is a type of comparative philology that I have never enjoyed and that I wish you would not enter into. Such weapons do not suit you..

Keep in mind as well that Elisha not an apostate merely because he was familiar with Greek literature. Three quarters of the ancient and modern Sages would be deemed so as well; it was for the reason that you know and that I need not tell you, the author of the *Vikkuaḥ*. As for "Greek tunes," if I am not mistaken, it was you yourself who interpreted this in the sense of erotic poetry or something of that sort. Am I wrong?...

I would like you to see in this letter a proof of my desire to be your friend, no more or less. If you justly speak of not fearing or hoping for anything from anyone, tell me now, why would I, your adversary, show you affection if I did not love you, especially for your studious self-sacrifice? What do I hope for or fear from you? But I would be a liar my whole life if I kept silent whenever I thought you spoke incorrectly....

Say to me something better than "most devoted," and believe me to be your most affectionate.

Eliyahu Benamozegh

Letter 4

Shadal to Rabbi Benamozegh

Date: Sept. 8, 1863

Most esteemed Sir,

...Your reflections have brought you to believe that
Mosaism without that theology [Kabbalah] is absolutely
lacking in basis. Now see whether we can be friends. I
have dedicated my life and my entire being to the
defence of simple Mosaism, which is and always was
understood by all of antiquity, while you aim for
nothing less than making it appear absurd and vain.
Christianity sought to do the same. But Christianity has
produced good outside the Synagogue. To the contrary,
the new Kabbalists, new but worse Christians, tend to
attack the Synagogue without benefiting any other
people. You, in order to be consistent, will take the field
with all those accusations that Christianity typically
makes against material Mosaism. What does Christianity

typically produce, when preached to the Jews? Vacillation in faith in some, faith in Christianity in none. Today, Kabbalistic mysticism, preached in your sense, would have the same result.

Is this not a frightful abyss that you are digging between you and me? Are we not two opposite poles? Nevertheless, I do not wish to go to battle against you, for the age is too materialistic to allow the forces of mysticism to gain power against Mosaism, while you yourself, I hope, would never wish to imitate the Christians and make yourself an open adversary of the pure and straightforward material, civil, and political Mosaism. And if you would ever do such a thing, the institutions of Moses would still, even in our times, have valiant apologists, and the very consonance of your objections with those so often repeated by the followers of the Nazarene would be sufficient to render them innocuous to our coreligionists.

Besides, can you believe that you have refuted me? You yourself say that your work is not finished. Have you said a word against the most evident proofs of the non-antiquity of the Zohar?...

Without wishing to call you a charlatan or a writer in bad faith, I can believe you to be convinced that you have created a pious work defending to the best of your ability a doctrine that you can believe to be salutary and necessary for the correction of the current materialism.

...I am not disgusted with you, nor am I ever disgusted with a person for personal motives. But the principle professed by you, the absurdity of material Mosaism (which I adore and for which I sacrifice myself), does not permit me to declare you (without hypocrisy) a friend....

Polemics with Christianity have never stirred my blood. If someone came to attack me, I would respond, "The swords still exist; they have not yet been turned into plowshares." So no one has come. "But be a good Christian," [I say,] "and let everyone be faithful to their native beliefs." It was in this sense that I often spoke with Monsignor Nardi, when he was a professor here, and we lived for many years in good harmony.[52]

---

[52] Monsignor Francesco Nardi (1808-1877) was a Professor of Canon Law at the University of Padua. An obituary described him as "one of the most indefatigable, earnest, and even violent defenders of the cause of the Pope," but it went on to observe that "no difference in political opinions, even the most diametrically opposite, ever interfered with the affection and esteem for those whom he had once reckoned among his old friends" (*Proceedings of the Royal Geographic Society*, London, 1877, pp. 426-427). In an 1839 monograph on the history of embroidery, Nardi acknowledges Shadal's assistance in furnishing biblical references and calls him "an ornament of our city" (*Sull' origine dell' arte del ricamo*, Padua, 1839, p. 19). In 1847, he and Shadal served together on a commission to decipher a supposedly ancient bronze tablet that

Live in happiness for many, many years, and always
believe me to be

Your most devoted,
S. D. L.

faithful to the plain truths
unmixed with fables;
friend of peace
even with the mysticists,
even with the Christians.[53]

---

had been discovered in Sicily (*Epistolario*, pp. 514–515). In an 1850
letter to Nardi (*Epistolario*, p. 585), Shadal takes issue with a point
that Nardi made in a book about the "truth of the Catholic religion"
(see note 26 below). But seven years later, another letter from Shadal
to Nardi opens with the salutation *Chiarissimo professore, amico
carissimo* ("Most distinguished professor, dearest friend"), followed
by a discussion of Genesis ch. 14 and certain Hebrew and Arabic
Dead Sea–related place names (*Epistolario*, pp. 916–917). Shadal
closes this letter with *di Lei devotissimo amico* ("your most devoted
friend").

[53] In Italian, the last two lines share a rhythm and rhyme: *anche coi
misticisti / anche coi gesucristi.*

Letter 5

Rabbi Benamozegh to Shadal

Date: Sept. 12, 1863

Most esteemed Sir and Friend,

...If I am to judge from certain phrases in your letter... it would seem that I am nothing less than a Christianiser, who wishes to deviate from that which all of antiquity understood as the Mosaic faith. But what is this antiquity for which you reserve a privilege? Is it the Mosaic antiquity? And would you call the Mosaic antiquity "simple"?... But you know very well that simplicity is not a legitimate mark of a true religion, for the truth by its nature is complex, organic, harmonic, nor is Mosaism a simple thing in this sense of simplicity. Material Mosaism, as you call it—does it seem simple to you?... The religious laws, ceremonies, rituals that regulate the relationship between humankind and God and which provide the primary criteria for correctly judging the nature of a religion—do they seem simple to you?... That immense, multiform body of practices and rites, however it may be explained, can it exist together with that meagre Deism that wants to attach itself to the majestic Jewish organism, like the head of a dwarf to the body of a giant? Can you deny that even in the Talmudic tradition there is an esoteric knowledge?

S. D. L. is too much a person of good faith to try to deny it. You will say that those mysteries did exist, to be sure, but that they disappeared and were taken over by false ones. But is there anything more unlikely than this? In such a short time? With hardly any interruption or vacancy of position, given that the last of the Amoraim were not far distant from the Geonim? Then you cannot allege that traditional antiquity consisted of simple Mosaism. Where is this antiquity, then? In R. Ḥai Gaon, who was a Kabbalist[54], in RaABa"D [R. Abraham ben David], in R. Eliezer the teacher of RaMBa"N, in RaMBa"N [Naḥmanides], in RaSHB"A [R. Shelomo ben

---

[54] Editor's note: It seems that some Kabbalists ascribed various Kabbalistic writings to Rabbenu Ḥai Gaon. However, as Steinschneider notes: *"Certain Kabbalistic pieces were ascribed to him [Ḥai Gaon]; but in truth he was no mystic in the usual sense of the word. In fact, he fought against superstition. He was an orthodox Jew, in possession of general culture, but hostile to deeper philosophical research."* ("Hebr. Uebers." p. 910) Further, the elements of the later Kabbalah not found in Talmudic tradition, such as the belief that miracles could be performed with the names of God, he designated as foolishness not credited by any sensible man.

Abraham ibn Aderet], in [R. Moses] Cordobero, in [R. Yosef] Qaro, in Abrabanel, in RaSHBa"S [R. Simeon ben Zemaḥ Duran], not to speak of a thousand other pureblooded Kabbalists? Will you say that these, too, are Mystics and Christians? You may say it and think it. As for me, I consider those named—let it not displease you— more authoritative masters of that which is Mosaism than any others, no matter how much learning and fame they may have in the world....

Who are the new Christians who aim to destroy the Synagogue? Who is it who is proclaiming the abolition of the Law as Jesus or his followers did? Certainly not the new Kabbalists, who, to the contrary, are closing off the way to any innovation... and elevating [religious] practice from a mere externality, from an insipid ceremonial... to a necessity of the highest order, to a cosmic, eternal, universal need... If by "Mosaism" you mean only the written law, this type of Mosaism will never suffice to satisfy the religious sentiment, if there is not united with it the dual tradition, that is, the practical (Mishnah-Talmud) and the speculative (Kabbalah). Indeed, the Kabbalah renders Christian propaganda useless and powerless, because it fills the immense void left by material Mosaism.

...Who ever thought or maintained that the Zohar did not contain interpolations, even large and copious ones? Did I not clearly say so in the *Ta'am le-*

89

Shad? Are there not, according to the Talmud, interpolations even in the Pentateuch (*Shemonah Pesuqim*)[55], and in the Talmud, the Mishnah, and the Midrashim are there not continuous and well-known interpolations? But why do you want to have two systems of weights and measures concerning the one and the other? And then— and then—if the truth were not impeding me, do you know that I would be capable of conceding to you that the Zohar is false from top to bottom, while nevertheless requiring you to agree that the Kabbalah is ancient? What does the Zohar have to do with the Kabbalah, the bibliographical question with the critical and theological question?... Yes, sir: there are interpolations in the Zohar; what of it? And if you insist— *ve-im takniteni*—I would add, yes sir, the Zohar is false; so what? The Kabbalah existed before it among the Amoraim, Geonim, Rabbanim, and it will exist after it.

At all costs, you do not want to declare yourself a friend to me.

And why? Because [you say] I assert the absurdity of material Mosaism. Do you mean to say "practical"? Then guard yourself from believing that I call it absurd, because you would be libelling me. It is precisely because I do not call it absurd that I attribute to it a spirit, its own

---

[55] That is, the final eight verses of the Torah, relating the death of Moses. According to a Tannaitic opinion cited in *Baba Batra* 15a, Joshua wrote these verses.

contemporaneous twin theory, which is the Kabbalah. There once was a mysticism that despised practice, and that was the mysticism of the Kabbalist Jesus, who abolished the law—and that of Shabbetai Ṣebi, another Kabbalist Jesus, who declared himself superior to it, as you know—but this is not mine. Mine is that of Naḥmanides, of those who entered the *Pardes* (except for Elisha),[56] of R. Ḥai Gaon, the RaSHB"A, the RaSHBa"S, R. Yosef Qaro, R. Cordobero, the Ari [R. Isaac Luria], and all that beautiful school of thought that raised up the value of practice.

And on the day that I come to imitate the Kabbalist Jesus or Shabbetai Ṣebi and violate the material Mosaism that I adore as you do and in which I take delight in fulfilling the practical miṣvot, I will say as I said fifteen years ago in my first sermon, *tivash yadi ve-en yemini kahoh tikh'heh*[57]....

Perhaps you are dubious about me, seeing that I have neglected the defence of the Written Torah and the Oral

---

[56] "The Rabbis taught: Four entered the *Pardes* ['the orchard,' i.e., Heaven]. They were Ben Azzai, Ben Zoma, Aḥer [Elisha ben Abuyah], and Rabbi Aqiba... Ben Azzai gazed [at the Divine Presence] and died... Ben Zoma gazed and was harmed [he lost his sanity]... Aḥer cut down the plantings [he became a heretic]. Rabbi Aqiba came out safely" (*Ḥagigah* 14b).

[57] "May my arm be withered, and my right eye utterly darkened"—a paraphrase of Zekhariah 11:17.

Torah, strictly speaking, and have taken a fancy to the Kabbalah, but the reason is clear:

1. Because in my opinion, the Kabbalah contains the principles, the theory of the Written Torah and the Oral Torah, and once the principles are defended, the consequences are validated.

2. Because it is the more mistreated one, and I have a secret inclination toward causes that are unfortunate but true. You may even call me, if you will, an advocate of lost causes. That is my character, enough said. I consider the Kabbalah to be a *met miṣva she-en lo koberim* [i.e., an unattended dead body with no one to bury it], whose care takes precedence over all other obligations.

I tell you this because I have been looked upon with similar doubts by others, and to all of them I have replied the same.

Why, then, do you not want to call me a friend? We both believe in God, in the Mosaic revelation; may I say, also in the tradition? For the love of Heaven, do not tell me no. Then what difference remains between us? That you do not believe that the Kabbalah is part of Mosaism, and that I believe it. We are both of good faith, but let us guard ourselves against being intolerant; excuse the term and do not take any offence. Would you not feel capable of being a friend to a Christian, to a Deist, to a Karaite, as long as they were of good faith? I myself feel capable of doing so, and I have had and still have several such friends, whom I have instinctively considered adversaries before getting to know them, and afterwards I have valued and loved. If Naḥmanides were alive, would you not throw yourself into his arms, and would you not kiss his hand? Would you tell him, too, that he is not your friend? Let us imagine, then, what you would say to the Rambam [Maimonides], who Aristotelises Mosaism—and it is he who in fact partly disfigures its fair face. I stop my ears so as not to hear it. Ah, but the holy Naḥmanides did not act this way; great Kabbalist (and Christian?) that he was, he took up against everyone the defence of—who? Of one who, like you, stood at the opposite pole of Kabbalism—of the Rambam. Although old and dying, he went wandering from city to city to save the Rambam from infamy and his books from the flames. And the Christian Benamozegh, he swears to God that he would know how to do as much for S. D. L. if another Philippson tried to stain his reputation,[58] and if the Orthodox defamed

---

[58] Ludwig Philippson (1811-1889) was a Reform Jewish journalist and scholar in Germany, founder and editor of the *Allgemeine Zeitung des Judentums*. Benamozegh may be referring to an article in this journal (vol. 21, no. 48, Nov. 23, 1857, pp. 657-659) in which Philippson subjected Shadal to a lengthy and savage attack, saying

him for faults that he does not have. And he would do so more worthily and meritoriously than the crowd of admirers who swear upon his every word and who know how to say nothing but amen. I would add *yehe shemeh rabba meborakh* to all (and it is a great deal) that you have well said....

It would be wrong, then, for you to refuse to declare yourself my friend. I would not care so much if it were a millionaire [who was so refusing], but you, whose abnegation and sincerity I admire, I must care about; and that same ingenuous declaration of not wanting to be my friend—in an age in which *affezionatissimi* and *sviceratissimi* [i.e., insincere declarations of "most affectionate" and "passionately yours"] rain down like roof tiles on one's head—makes me love you all the more. I am like those women who fall ever more deeply in love with one who makes a show of not loving or caring for them. What can one do? Everyone has his own tastes....

Polemics with Christianity do not please you. It is certainly more convenient not to conduct them. But they are necessary for the fate of future humanity. How

---

among other things, "The ridiculous vanity and self-worship of this great Italian *Havdolos-Fabrikant* is known to everyone." Philippson's colorful Hebrew- German epithet, literally "manufacturer of distinctions," has been understood as "philological hairsplitter" (Margolies, *Samuel David Luzzatto*, p. 53).

unfortunate for us if our predecessors in the world had fled from polemics! We would still be at the level of fetishism. You say, "If someone came to attack me, I would respond," etc. But when the arena is open and there is publishing and printing, the attack and the defence must be permanent. When there was no printing, or when it existed but with the counterweight of the Inquisition, I understand that the Jews would have had to wait for the knock on the doors of the synagogue and be pulled by their pigtails before responding. But today! Certainly tact, moderation, and prudence are necessary, but one must do battle. Otherwise Judaism will be taken away; it is not enough to say that it is divine and therefore immortal, because we are not speaking of Judaism per se; rather, we are speaking of Judaism in the hearts and minds of the people, and that can go away. Truth and virtue, too, are divine and immortal; is that a reason why one should not exert all one's efforts to make people better and more fully educated? Without a doubt this is not the way to live peacefully in the world; rather, it is an obligation that must be fulfilled.

One thing, I cannot deny, has surprised me. Can you really say, "Be a good Christian and let everyone be faithful to their native beliefs"? It must be one of two things: either you said this in order to flee from bother and disturbance—and I can sympathise, but this is not a system to build oneself as a rule—or you said it in good faith, and in that case it is religious indifferentism,[59] for it is as if to say that if all the religions cannot be equally good and true, it follows that they are all equally false. Moreover, would it not be a grave sin to speak this way to a tritheist, a Christian, if it is not for the sake of fleeing from danger? *Ve-lifne ivver lo titten mikhshol* ["Do not place a stumbling block before the blind"—Lev. 19:14]. What I ask of you is not to live with me in good harmony as you lived with Monsignor Nardi. Let my "nard" send forth to you a different scent: *nirdi natan reḥo*[60]—not to live with me in that sort of peace in which you are disposed to live with Christians; good politics, no doubt, but not what I would want you to employ with me.[61]

---

[59] The term "indifferentism" is used in Catholic teaching to refer to the mistaken belief that no one religion or philosophy is superior to another.

[60] "My nard sent forth its fragrance"—Song of Songs 1:12. Nard (*nerd* in Hebrew) is a flowering plant of the honeysuckle family that yields spikenard, a perfume oil.

[61] As noted above, however (see footnote 18), Shadal did not shy away from asserting religious disagreement with Nardi on at least one occasion. In a note on p. 239 of Nardi's book *Verità della religione naturale e cristiana cattolica* ("The Truth of the Natural and Christian Catholic Religion," Padua, 1840), Nardi had said that "the idea that God could suffer and die would be opposed to reason, but not that a Person uniting in himself, to be sure in an incomprehensible manner, the divine nature with the human could, like a man, be born, suffer, die, and rise again." In a letter to Nardi

...I believe that we can still come to an understanding, that we can each make reciprocal concessions, and on the day in which we present ourselves to the world united together, and by dint of good will and love of the truth we combine together the *Vikkuah* and the *Ta'am le-Shad*, then I believe I will hear in the distance a different braying from the one that you heard in my pamphlet—the braying of the donkey of the King Messiah.

...Tomorrow you will hear the shofar and I will hear it. What will that sound say to you? Your material Mosaism, what will it say to you? Surely nothing other than one of the charming but puerile reasons that have been given outside of the Kabbalah, and to hear it with devotion, to give importance to the *teki'ah, shevarim, teru'ah*, will require of you an extraordinary effort of faith. For me, as you know, the matter is quite different. Every note has its importance, just as every atom of material is a mystery, just as every physical object has its

---

dated June 25, 1850 (*Epistolario*, p. 585), Shadal expressed the view that one's "eternal health" cannot depend on "the acceptance of incomprehensible dogmas. God can indeed demand of us the sacrifice of our passions, but never that of our sound reason.... This, reduced to the most basic terms, is the Jewish-Christian question. In a word, a Jew does not find the Note on p. 239 convincing." It is significant that Shadal refused to accept "incomprehensible" ideas from Christianity and Kabbalism alike.

place and value in Creation. For me, the Torah is the prototype of the world, it is the world in the mind of God, it is the true incarnate word of the *miṣvot ha-ma'asiyyot*. What does it seem to you? Am I or am I not a devoted friend of material Mosaism? But with a slight difference from you.

And when I hear the shofar tomorrow, I too will say, "Let S. D. L. live many, many happy years; God spare him further suffering so that his mind may be kept serene and strong in the cultivation of sacred literature, and so that if one day he, too, decides to be a Christian like Rabbi Aqiba and Naḥmanides, he will be able to direct his potent scholarship to the triumph of the Truth." I too say, "Live many years," but I do not add the restricted complimentary close of "most devoted"; rather, I say, with a love that I pray to God is the same for me as I feel for you, O good and brave Luzzatto, at this moment,

Most lovingly yours,

Eliyahu Benamozegh

Letter 6

Shadal to Rabbi Benamozegh

Date: Sept. 18, 1863

Most esteemed friend,

...I will tell you that the trills of the shofar were (as I believe) commanded by God to put into public notice (at a time when no calendars were printed) the beginning of the year, just as on the tenth day of the year, with the same shofar, the arrival of the Jubilee year was brought into universal awareness. If today such sounds have lost their [original] purpose, they still preserve (as do so many ceremonies) the immense value of reminding us of our ancient political existence, and they revive in us the feeling of nationality, which— without so many small but repeated reminders—perhaps might have become extinct among us, as it did among all the other ancient nations. Those trills excite in me clear ideas, profound sensations, the most edifying reflections. The miracle of our existence animates me, it encourages me to endure in the struggle against Spinoza,[62] against all the supposedly enlightened ones, and to risk everything, whatever may occur, in defence of a cause that has been victorious until now and that will certainly remain victorious.

To me, that horn is the drum of nationality, of the existence of a people that was once a nation and that today lives only in God, and that will cease to exist only when it ceases to believe in God.

I now take in hand the *Mishnat Ḥasidim* of the unfortunate Ricchi,[63] and I search therein for the mysterious value of those trills, and I understand nothing of it. But I suppose that others do understand it, and I equally suppose (for the moment) that there is a real and

---

[62] Benedict (Baruch) Spinoza was Shadal's particular *bête noire*. See, for example, his commentary to Exod. 15:3: "According to Spinoza, everything that exists in the world is of necessity, and not at all a matter of will; but according to the Jews (from Abraham until today), nothing exists of necessity, and everything is a product of God's will. The faith of Spinoza and the faith of the Hebrews are as distant from each other as east and west, and the opposition of one to the other is total."

[63] Immanuel Ḥai Ricchi (1688-1743) was an Italian rabbi and Kabbalist who was killed by robbers (hence Shadal's description of him as "unfortunate"). *Mishnat Ḥasidim* (Amsterdam, 1727), considered his most important book, is an intricate Kabbalistic work that contains a subdivision devoted to *kavvanot*, or mystical meditations.

true interaction between the two worlds, and that true and quite real are all the celestial and more than celestial effects of those trills. Then I ask myself, those who groundlessly call Mosaism "literal," with its precepts that have no motivation other than being *gezerat ha-melekh* ("the King's decree"), do they have anything better? Granted all their mysterious motives for the Mosaic precepts, have they taken one step forward, do they have some more advanced theory than the one which we all know—that is, that "God has commanded that which He desired"?

Fools! They do not know that the ultimate reason for all things is the Divine good pleasure,[64] and that on earth and in Heaven, everything that has happened could have happened in a completely different manner, if the Creator had been otherwise pleased. If our trills electrify and put in motion the most exalted worlds, that happens only through the Divine good pleasure; any reason beyond this one does not exist, and cannot exist. And so no matter how many mysteries may be invented, nothing will ever go beyond the *gezerat ha-melekh*.

Besides, the notion that one's execution of the Divine precepts must be accompanied by sublime

---

[64] Italian *beneplacito*. Its French equivalent, *bon plaisir*, appears in a phrase once used by monarchs when signing a law: *Car tel est notre bon plaisir* ("For such is our good pleasure").

meditations [*kavvanot*] is never stated in the Law, and the ancient Rabbis disputed as to whether the precepts can be fulfilled only if they are carried out with *kavvanah*. Such *kavvanah* is not that of the mystics, but is the simple consciousness of executing a Divine precept. And if not even such consciousness was believed to be necessary by some of the great Sages, who would dare to deny the epithet of "Orthodox" to one who cannot agree that the material execution of the Divine precepts is nothing if it is unaccompanied by mysterious *kavvanot*?

Metaphysical delusions are certainly ancient. But our Masters knew of their futility and evil consequences, and they lamented, *"Anyone who speculates about four things [it would have been better if he had not come into the world: what is above, what is below, what was before, and what will be after]."*[65] Thus they did not profess any doctrine that purported to scrutinise the incomprehensible. They were not so foolish as to ask why the world was created when it was, and not before or after that time, only to respond (see *Eṣ Ḥayyim, Hekhal*

---

[65] The citation is from Mishna *Ḥagigah* 2:1. The *Tiferet Yisrael* commentary explains this statement as a warning against speculation as to what is beyond space and time, since such matters are beyond human understanding, and seeking such knowledge will lead to error and heresy.

1, Gate 1, Branch 2)[66] that the present lower world could have existed only after the creation of all the other worlds above it, which came into existence one after the other— without realising that the Creator, Who was in existence an eternity ago, could have begun His work some millions of centuries previously or subsequently, as He wished, and that the moment in which our world's existence became possible could have been brought forward or backward by some millions of centuries without any why or wherefore, for the eternal and unique Being has no one on whom to depend, and there can be no other why or wherefore than His own good pleasure.

Most wisely, our Masters gave the label of *"one who has no consideration for the honour of his Maker"* to such metaphysicians [Mishnah Ḥagigah 2:1], who pose absurd questions and resolve them with answers that are even more absurd. Such questions and such answers were not handed down by them to us, because they

---

[66] *Eṣ Ḥayyim* (1573) is a Kabbalistic work based on a compilation of the teachings of R. Isaac Luria by R. Ḥayyim Vital (1542-1620). "Anyone who enters the complex world of the *Eṣ Ḥayyim*... will quickly realise that these are texts which have little regard for Scripture and are not founded on what we may call normative rabbinic and/or the early theosophic Kabbalistic tradition." (Magid, Shaul. "From Theosophy to Midrash: Lurianic Exegesis and the Garden of Eden," *AJS Review*, Vol. 22, No. 1. New York: 1997, p. 38).

declared themselves openly opposed to such impertinences. These cannot be traced back to the Mosaic revelation, because they are absurd, and if they could be traced back to that source, they would have been respected by the ancient Masters.

These ancient Sages of ours, who did not permit the Oral Law to be written down—would they ever have dreamed of entrusting to paper, or allowing others to write down, the arcane doctrines that they confided only to their most experienced disciples? Is it possible that Simeon bar Yoḥai could actually have given the order, *"Rabbi Abba will write [the secrets of the Torah]"?*[67]

If fanaticism allows itself to see here and there in the Zohar a few egregious outliers[68] and to admit to the presence of a few interpolations, the dispassionate observer finds that the book contains not even half a page that could possibly belong to those personages to whom it is attributed. And if, then, a Kabbalist wanted to renounce the Zohar and keep the Kabbalah, he could absolutely not do so, for his inspired men— Isaac Luria, Joseph Qaro, and whoever else there may be—all

[67] This is a reference to the *Idra Zuta*, a portion of the Zohar (*Ha'azinu*) describing a gathering of Rabbi Shimon bar Yoḥai's students on the day of his death, at which time it is said that he told Rabbi Abba to write down the secret Torah teachings that he had not previously revealed to them.

[68] Italian *farfalloni*, literally "butterflies" and idiomatically "philanderers."

accepted the Zohar as a work of the Masters whose names it bears, and so they would all be false prophets. Would that Kabbalist want to renounce even Luria and go back to Naḥmanides? We will talk then.

I cannot examine your lengthy book, which I read with great effort only once. It will suffice for me to let you know that my aversion to Kabbalah does not stem from incredulity or heterodoxy, but is a profound religious sentiment. It will suffice for me to let you know that it would be quite easy for me to rebut the *Ta'am le-Shad*, and that I do not do so in order to avoid wasting time, since mysticism itself is too contrary to the spirit of the age, with its partisans becoming scarcer every day.

If you defend mysticism, I will let you do it; if you speak ill of me, I will let you do it. Can you call for more friendship than this?

You want to be my friend, but at the same time you would like to see me converted. And I evade missionaries. Friend or not, you know me as an honest man, ready to be of service to you sincerely, more than many professed friends.

I will add, to avoid any misunderstanding, that by "simple and material Mosaism" I mean, for example, sounding the shofar, or hearing it sounded, without engaging in mystical *kavvanot* [meditations], but with the sole *kavvanah* [intention] of fulfilling a Divine precept, which is holy for us for the simple reason that it was imposed upon us by God, and which had its social purposes in the Israelite republic, but which for us, in our dispersion, is a religious ceremony that sanctifies us and brings us closer to God (see *Lezioni di Teologia morale*, §§ 21, 29).[69]

One who defends the *kavvanot* defends doctrines of which not a trace is found in the Mishnah or Talmud; and one who, in so doing, considers himself Orthodox is a fanatic, which can be tolerated. But one who dares to declare heterodox someone who does not think of such things as he does—he is impertinent and insults without any shade of reason our entire antiquity, which never knew anything of *kavvanot*, and in which great and venerable Masters denied even that precepts can be fulfilled only with *kavvanah*.

Having now re-read your letter, I find that I must respond to the objections that you make to my remark, "Be a good Christian."

This is not politics, and it is not indifferentism. I am convinced that Christianity is not a polytheism.

---

[69] This book ("Lessons in Moral Theology"), published by Shadal in Padua, 1862, states in § 21 that the laws relating to the service of God serve the purpose of keeping the idea of God and Providence in our minds, as a means of keeping us honest and virtuous. In § 29, Shadal emphasises that the ceremonial laws never lose this beneficial effect and thus continue to merit observance, even though many of them were originally intended to distance the Israelites from idolatry.

Christianity professes one single God, and its first followers suffered martyrdom for not worshipping "the gods."

The mysteries with which it defaces pure monotheism are errors, but it does not thereby cease to be a monotheism. It is a calumny, an iniquity, to declare a person to be a polytheist or a tritheist if that person sincerely wants to be and believes himself to be a monotheist. Convinced that the world does not have to become Jewish and will not, at some time, have to become circumcised, I want the Christian to live as a good Christian and be faithful to the evangelical morality, and not—in renouncing Christ—to renounce Moses, renounce God, and worship Spinoza.[70]

---

[70] It would seem that later in life, Benamozegh's attitude toward Christianity underwent a change. Consider the following passage from an English translation of *Israël et l'Humanité*, a work edited by Aimé Pallière from Benamozegh's notes after his death: "And now we turn to the followers of the two great messianisms, Christian and Moslem. It is to Christians in particular that we wish to address a frank and respectful word, and God knows that it is with fear in our heart lest our advances be taken for hypocrisy. No! No impartial and reasonable man can fail to recognize and appreciate, as is appropriate, the exalted worth of these two great religions, more especially of Christianity. There is no Jew worthy of the name who does not rejoice in the great transformation wrought by them in a world formerly defiled…As for ourselves, we have never had the experience of hearing the Psalms of David on the lips of a priest without feeling such sensations. The reading of certain passages of

Of God there is very little that we can comprehend, and I am quite tolerant, and you might say indifferent—or, if you like, an indifferentist—regarding theoretical errors when it comes to metaphysics. I would never have condemned or scorned our ancient anthropomorphists, nor would I have condemned Maimonides for his spiritualism; nor do I despise the Kabbalists for their beliefs, but they are my enemies when they insult non-mystical Mosaism, when they vilify the *peshat de-oraita*, the plain meaning of the Torah.

You see that our opinions are more than slightly in discord, and that we will never be able to come to agreement. But if in any case you want me as a friend, I will be one, as I am with so many others, always telling you the truth without a veil and without reticence.

...The Zohar says that Hoshana Rabbah is the *siyuma de-dina* ('the conclusion of judgement'), and yet you would make Shemini Aseret analogous to Yom Kippur, that is, the Day of Judgment. Is this not making a mockery of the Zohar and your readers?[71] And by

---

the Gospels has never left us unresponsive. The simplicity, grandeur, infinite tenderness, which these pages breathe out overwhelms us to the depths of our soul...." (Luria, Maxwell, trans. and ed. *Israel and Humanity*. New York: Paulist Press, 1995, pp. 50–51.)

[71] Here Shadal is criticising the opening section of *Ta'am le-Shad*, in which Benamozegh notes that the two protagonists of Shadal's

putting this argument at the front of your book, is this not as if it said:

> *Lasciate ogni speranza, voi ch'entrate,*
> *Di trovar qui sode ragioni e belle;*
> *Ma sofismi e menzogne imbelletate,*
> *E falso giorno e notte senza stelle—?*[72]

...Live happily and believe me to be Your sincere friend,

S. D. L.

P.S. You make mention of those who "entered the Pardes," as if they were Kabbalists. R. Ḥai [Gaon] had it by tradition that by means of certain preparations, they came to see the heavenly hosts. Thus, neither they nor he were Kabbalists in the modern sense, but they were all anthropomorphists, professing a material mysticism

---

Vikkuaḥ conducted their debate on the night of Hoshana Rabbah. This serves as a point of departure for an extended discussion between Benamozegh's own two protagonists (pp. 2–21) as to the Kabbalistic significance of Hoshana Rabbah and the holiday that immediately follows it, Shemini Aṣeret.

[72] Here Shadal has borrowed a famous line from Canto III of Dante's *Inferno* and added three more of his own devising. These lines may be translated as follows: *"All hope abandon, ye who enter here/ Of finding here firm and fair reasonings/ But only sophisms and painted fallacies/ And false day, and night without stars."*

which is that of the *Shiur Qomah*[73] and the *Pirqe Hekhalot*,[74] a doctrine that has fallen into discredit and practically into oblivion after the war waged by Maimonides against every form of *hagshamah* [i.e., belief in the corporeality of God].

The author of the Kuzari [Yehuda Halevi] contributed some words and ideas to the Zohar (see Munk, Gebirol, p. 277),[75] but he did not know the Kabbalah strictly speaking, for in the Sefirot he saw only abstract numerical ideas, never real substances, worlds, emanations, or what have you, like those of the Kabbalists, to which prayers are addressed. Steinschneider (Mazkir, p. 59)[76] gives you credit for

---

[73] A Midrashic work purporting to describe the measurements of God's bodily parts. Maimonides claimed that it was a heretical Byzantine-era forgery.

[74] Otherwise known as *Hekhalot Rabbati*, a work of uncertain date and authorship, in which Rabbi Ishmael relates how he, with a company of colleagues, learned the secrets of ascending to see "the King in His beauty."

[75] That is, Munk, Salomon. *Mélanges de philosophie Juive et Arabe.* Paris: 1857-1859, pp. 277-278. There, Munk asserts that the concept of Israel as the heart of all the nations was adopted by the Zohar from the *Kuzari*. Shadal refers to the book as "Gebirol" because its first part contains excerpts from Solomon ibn Gabirol's *Meqor Hayyim (Fons Vitae)*.

[76] Steinschneider, Moritz, ed. *Ha-Mazkir (Hebräische Bibliographie)*, vol. 5. Berlin: 1862. Founded in 1858, *Ha-Mazkir* was a bibliographical journal of Judaica that enumerated each year's literary publications. Shadal (who is listed as a contributor to the

attempting to show elements of the Kabbalah in the Kuzari, and then he adds, "It remains to be asked, however, how much of the Kuzari entered into the Kabbalah of the thirteenth century."

---

volume in question) is referring to a notice describing Benamozegh's *Ta'am le-Shad*.

Letter 7

Rabbi Benamozegh to Shadal

Date: Sept. 21, 1863

Most esteemed friend,

...You believe that the trills of the shofar were commanded by God to put into public notice, when no calendars were printed, the beginning of the year. Permit a few questions that my meagre intellect suggests:

1. Was it really necessary for God to reveal Himself in order to unveil this fine idea? Does it not seem to you that it would have been better for the Divine mind to have revealed some kind of signal that was unknown then and only put into practice afterward, since such a thing would have better verified the intervention of the Supreme Intellect?
2. How would the shofar have been more effective than a simple public announcement?

3. Why would practices such as this one have to be observed today, since, as you say, their purpose has ceased? Is it reasonable for people to be chained to inane practices, and—notwithstanding the bright light of civilization and a plethora of more befitting means— be petrified in antiquated and obsolete ways that can have nothing more than a simply archaeological value?

4. If they are practised today for no other reason than to remind us of our political existence, I ask: (1) What is the purpose, then, of all those rules, prescriptions, minute details that regulate the form, time, mode, and instrumentation of those sounds? (2) Are you not afraid that a rabbi who has been indoctrinated in these principles of yours, and who does not believe it precisely necessary to perpetuate the remembrance of bygone times, this empty ceremonial, might put a stop to these practices, among the most incomprehensible and alien of our customs, or at least suppress with a coup d'état all the *dinim* of the shofar and substitute some instrument, some sound, some form in its place?[77] (3) Furthermore,

---

[77] In fact, at one time, many Reform congregations dispensed with the shofar, perceiving it as "primitive sounding, raucous, informal, antiquated, and therefore inherently inappropriate to their religious aesthetics; many American Reform congregations simply

are you not afraid that some Italian or German reformer or deformer, starting out from your own premises, might say, "Better than this horn-blaring, a fine and unctuous sermon speaks to the heart and mind," thus lending authorization to the German Reform, which, it is well to remember, has been motivated by none other than this precise principle, that is—as you say— that this and so many other ceremonies have only a commemorative purpose? (4) And if this is true, what idea do you have of a wise God Who knows no better than to order this amorphous means of proclamation and then—with the progress of the times and human erudition in civil life—not only fails to sanction new and more fitting ideas by means of another revelation, but wishes His people to continue living in the temple of a semi-barbaric life of forty centuries ago, and Who permits and indeed wants them to say, *"Blessed be You, O Eternal, Who commanded us to hear the sound of the shofar"?...*

---

substituted a modern trumpet... while still others relied altogether on the organ's trumpet stop." (Levin, Neil W., liner notes to Herman Berlinski's *Shofar Service* (1999 recording), Milken Archive of Jewish Music, <https://www.milkenarchive.org/music/volumes/view/masterworks-of-prayer/work/shofar-service/>

I cannot discern that connection that you see between the sound of the shofar and our nationality. Does national life consist of perpetuating antiquated customs? A nation that has no current life and is reduced to feeding upon memories shows itself to be a nation no longer.

Furthermore, our nationality is a noble and sacred thing, no doubt, but nobler and holier is our religion; indeed, the former is no more significant than other nationalities if it does not serve as a means of perpetuating and augmenting the latter. To reduce the revealed precepts to mere national preservatives is to make them lose three quarters of their value; it is to reduce God to the rank of a Lycurgus or a Romulus[78]; it is to fuse religion, which can never die, with our nationality, which can; it is to expose religious truth to all those changes and vicissitudes and perils to which nationality is exposed; it is to say to the Jew, *"If you no longer care to live a separate national existence, you no longer have any reason to be observant";* it is to make eternity into a satellite of the present time.

Given the above, it cannot be understood why you so strongly condemn Spinoza, the enlightened ones, etc. For Spinoza thought precisely as you do with regard to the ceremonies and their origin and significance—

---

[78] In other words, a flesh-and-blood legislator. Lycurgus (fl. 820 BCE?) was the quasi-legendary lawgiver of Sparta, and Romulus was the legendary founder and first king of Rome.

only more logically and coherently than you, he made them human works, for truly there is no need for God to inconvenience Himself to do what you and I would have known to do. Spinoza and the enlightened ones have nothing against our nationality, but they are against our religion; and it is not an effective means of combating rationalism, pantheism, and illuminism to say to their advocates, *"God's precepts are nothing but national commemorative institutions and are simply ceremonial."*...

As for your declaration, "Fools! They do not know that the ultimate reason for all things is the Divine good pleasure": "Of course," say these fools, but they add, "Such good pleasure is not without great wherefores"; in other words, God's intelligence cannot be separated from His will, and one would truly be a fool if one were to make the Divine will into an idea similar to the *bon plaisir* of the French despots....

What you mean by "metaphysical delusions" I truly cannot say. Metaphysics is one of the primary needs of the human mind, and every time the mind reflects on things that are not physical bodies, that is metaphysics, like it or not. Woe to humanity if it could not occupy itself with metaphysical matters, but only with physical bodies and the relationships among them! Is this the material Judaism that you adore, that is, religious scepticism and obscurantism? You are frank with me; allow me to be so with you....If, when reading the *Ta'am le-Shad*, all hope is abandoned at the entrance, as you say, then when reading the *Vikkuah*, it is abandoned at the exit....

I have been reading these days, in the Maggid, your long and sensible reflections on Mendelssohn and his disciples.[79] You investigate with great sorrow how it was that from such a religious man was derived a school of sceptics, rationalists, and worse; and there passes in review an infinite number of causes that seem not to fully satisfy you, nor, truth be told, can they be satisfying. The true reason was too close to you for you to see it. Remember what I said to you in the pages above, that when it is established as a premise that in Mosaism there is nothing but *peshat*, when one denies absolute reasons for the precepts, independent of times or places, the consequences sooner or later are inevitable. This is what Mendelssohn did, and even if he did so with not quite as much solemnity as you do, certainly his inclinations with respect to *sod* [that is, esotericism] were not dissimilar to yours. See, now, the consequences. Those political, geographical, social, and moral motives that the *pashtanim* assign to the precepts do not stand up to analysis, to criticism, to human needs, interests, or passions. If one wants to preserve the *misvot*, they must be put on a higher plane in which these influences

---

[79] See *Ha-Maggid*, Sept. 17, 1863, p. 293; Sept. 24, p. 301.

cannot make themselves heard, and this is the plane of the absolute. Otherwise, Mendelssohn and Luzzatto, by sentiment, habit, personal persuasion, and pious and generous heart, will be pious, observant models of moral and religious virtue, but not being able to transmit these felicitous inclinations to those who succeed them, they will sooner or later have disciples who will draw out the consequences of their premises, who will say, "If the purpose of the Sabbath is only rest and a reminder of the creation, would it not be all the same to celebrate it a day later? Must we encounter thousands of sacrifices of interests, separate ourselves from the majority, cut ourselves off from the universal for a difference that amounts to nothing? If one eats *maṣah* for no other reason than the memory of the blessed unleavened dough, can we not remember it equally well with a good sermon, without submitting our teeth and stomach to torture for seven days? And above all, are they not ridiculous, those many minute precautions with which that bread is prepared?" I challenge a reasoning mind to stop the mouth of these terrible logicians and nevertheless to stay with the *peshat* exclusively.

The example of Mendelssohn seems to be made especially for you. If you do not pay heed in time, my prediction will be in vain, and you will be the Mendelssohn of our age in Italy and the rest of Europe. This is what you will be in delayed effect, just as you already are now in scholarship, fame, and inclinations. You who love Judaism, who I believe would give his life's blood for it—why would you want to leave within your mind this fatal germ that will bring forth its bitter fruits, perhaps when neither you nor I are in this world any longer to weep for it and remedy it? Do you want to see the advance signs now? Observe on whose side are the reformist aspirations, on your side or mine—that is to say, on the side of those who deny the Kabbalah like you, or of those who continue to accept it, relatively few to be sure (as you rejoice to say, with a joy that makes me shudder), but those who still remain. I would like to serve you in the manner of the squire of Xerxes, who said to him every morning when he awoke, "Sire, remember the Greeks." And I would like to whisper in your ear, "Remember Mendelssohn!"

I know how sterile this polemic of letters would be with anyone else, and I would not waste my time with one who was not capable of everything for the love of the true and the good. But I am writing to Luzzatto, to the man who... [could] make himself a hundred times greater than he is, becoming—as I said many years ago in L'Univers Israélite—after Moses, Ezra, and Hillel, the fourth restorer of our religion....

See that I speak to you with my heart on my lips and without reticence. I believe that in so doing, I will merit your friendship all the more.... This letter, which was begun before Yom Kippur, I finish today as Shemini Aṣeret has gone. Show yourself more solicitous than I am, and honour me more promptly with your response. Always most devotedly and affectionately yours,

Benamozegh

Letter 8

Rabbi Benamozegh to Shadal

Date: February 24, 1864

Most esteemed friend,

At this time I do not doubt that you have received the Vayiqra,[80] the sending of which was delayed by a day. You will find your interpretations cited in many places, sometimes disputed, other times approved and endorsed, always, I believe, with respect, and I regret it wherever I have not shown enough.[81] Here, too, you will find much

---

[80] That is, the Leviticus volume of *Torat HaShem*, Benamozegh's edition of the Pentateuch, including his commentary *Em LaMiqra* (Livorno, 1863).

[81] Benamozegh's first comment, on Lev. 1:2, would certainly have aroused Shadal's ire. He cites Shadal's opinion, in *Ha-Mishtadel*, that the idea of offering sacrifices to God originated not from a divine command, but from human impulses, and that the Torah—whose purpose was not to teach the people wisdom and knowledge, but to guide them on the paths of righteousness—did not abolish this custom. However, Benamozegh asserts not only that this opinion

that can be restated about the Kabbalah, which is our Helen—and as for which one of us is Menelaus and which one is Paris, I will leave the choice to you.[82] Only please, let there not break out between us a ten-year war, of which new Homers would have to sing after us: *"Cantami, o Diva, del pelide Achille le ire funeste/ che infiniti addusse lutti agli Achei."*[83]

I hope at least that you do me the justice of agreeing that my opinions are reasoned and serious. Why do you not write me more often? Writing itself can be a form of study, and if you do not care to continue our Kabbalistic polemic, is there any lack of subjects on which we can exchange our ideas? I do not know how

---

was mistaken, but that Shadal failed to perceive that he was following in the path of one whom he rightly despised, namely Spinoza, and that the same approach had been taken by the Christians and the leaders of the Reform movement.

[82] As recounted in Homer's *Iliad*, the beautiful Helen of Troy was the wife of Menelaus, king of Sparta, and was abducted by Paris, son of the king of Troy. This act was one of the immediate causes of the ten-year Trojan War. Benamozegh gives her name in the Italian form, "Elena." There is probably no way to know for certain whether Benamozegh was aware of it, but Elena (Leah in Hebrew) was in fact the name of Shadal's wife! In any case, Benamozegh's attempt at humour here may have fallen flat.

[83] "Sing, goddess, the anger of Peleus' son Achilles/ and its devastation, which put pains thousandfold upon the Achaians." These are the opening lines of the *Iliad* (trans. Richmond Lattimore, 1951). Benamozegh quotes the Italian version by Vincenzo Monti (1810).

much delight you might derive from it, but I do know
that I would enjoy it infinitely, since here one lives, or at
least I live, in a nearly perfect solitude, and except for the
company of my books, my children, and my new
students, I will tell you that now I see few people and
visit no one. What is more, I live in a villa and I am a
villano ["peasant"] all year. It can be said of me that I am
a field mouse, and that if you accept me as a table-mate
at the banquet of learning and friendship, the "feast of
the Leviathan," I can also be one who is *oleh al shulḥan
melakhim.*[84]

...[Teaching my new students] is a labour that is
taking ever greater proportions. God give me strength,
and may He give it to you, our Italian Nestor, as He
would to anyone who strives for goodness and truth.

I repeat then: write me and let us reason together
by letter as we would do verbally if we saw each other in
person. But what need is there to keep in mind what
divides us? Let us concentrate on what unites us and, in
our discussions, let us seek to eliminate any remaining
division. And I am, without any reservation, as always,
your most affectionate and devoted friend,

Benamozegh

---

[84] This is a jocular reference to a statement in *Aboda Zara* 68b that a
field mouse (as opposed to a city mouse) is considered a delicacy and
is *oleh al shulḥan shel melakhim* ("is served at the table of kings").

Letter 9

Rabbi Benamozegh to Shadal

Date: March 18, 1864

Most esteemed friend,

You so tight-fisted with letters and I so extravagant! This shows how much you are worth, and how little I am. Are you perhaps less than content with the somewhat free way that I treat your opinions in *Em LaMiqra*? I do not believe that I have ever fallen short of the respect due to you, but when one is as honest and of good faith as you are, one must understand that others who are equally convinced to the contrary may sometimes put slightly too much energy into defending their opinions. I have no need to praise you, but the esteem that I have for your learning and above all for your scholarly honesty makes me wish for you to care for me as much as I love you. Reading yesterday your response to Pineles in Ha-

Maggid,[85] I said, "Poor me! Must I, too, have aroused your anger?" For if I am not mistaken, on one occasion I wrote in *Em LaMiqra*, "In *Ha-Mishtadel*, the Scriptures have been distorted"; I said "*In Ha-Mishtadel*" [the title of your work, instead of referring to you by name], to be sure, to avoid defaming your name, but otherwise the signs of my esteem and the affection that I bear for you are not lacking. I would like to tell you here about my opinion of your response to Pineles, but I am avoiding a discussion for fear of writing 20-page letters and, what is worse, not receiving a reply....

One word about your response to Pineles. You oppose this writer, and rightly so, when he says that the Torah could suppress the instinct for revenge only up to a certain point. But oh, most honest Luzzatto! Do you not do the same? For what is that power left to—or that obligation imposed upon—the *go'el ha-dam*, whether

---

[85] Hirsch Mendel Pineles (1805-1870) was a Galician scholar. In the March 9, 1864 edition of *Ha-Maggid* [p. 77], Shadal defends his view, which Pineles had criticised, that an unintentional manslayer who leaves a city of refuge may be killed only by a particular blood-avenger (*go'el ha-dam*) and not by any member of the public at large. Shadal says, "If the words of the scholar Pineles had merely wounded my honour, I would have kept silent (as I have kept silent a number of times and have not responded to those who asserted empty claims against me, so as not to waste my time), but those words inflict a not inconsiderable injury upon the honour of our Torah, so how can I keep silent?" Note that Shadal's statement echoes the wording of his letter to Benamozegh of August 1863.

one person or a hundred, to shed the blood of the unintentional manslayer if not (under the system of pure *peshat*) a concession to the concepts and customs of the times? Can you maintain that a well-ordered society could tolerate similar abuses? Therefore it seems to me that between you and Pineles there is only a difference of degree. He makes the greater concession, you the lesser, but the system is entirely...

[Translator's note: Unfortunately, this is all we have of Rabbi Benamozegh's last letter. In his introduction to the Lettere volume, p. 4, Rabbi Benamozegh apologises for the truncation, and he explains that the original letter, which Shadal's sons had returned to him, had been misplaced, and that the only available copy was incomplete.]

Letters Between

Rabbi Abraham Yitzḥak Kook
&
Rabbi Yiḥya Qafiḥ

Translated by Ben Rothstein

Translator's Note

I have attempted to maintain the sense of the letters as written, with the peculiarities of Hebrew syntax intact except where this would greatly impede the understanding. I have kept footnotes to a minimum to facilitate smooth reading of the letters. Where the authors themselves provide a reference, this may be included in the main body text but supplemented with the full reference. (Parentheses) indicate bracketed passages in the original, [brackets] indicate editor's supplement to the text, and {braces} indicate text supplemented by one of the authors themselves. Finally, a degree of familiarity with the subject matter at hand is assumed, and so certain kabbalistic terms are left untranslated.

Ben Rothstein

Letter 1

Rabbi Kook to Rabbi Qafiḥ

Date: 26ᵗʰ Ṭebet 5691 [15ᵗʰ January 1931]

To the honourable great Rabbi, distinguished among men, who checks and examines the foundations and roots, our teacher Rabbi Yiḥya b. Suleiman al-Qafiḥ *SHLIṬ"A*, a greeting and holy blessing!

A letter of his dear eminence[86] has reached me, and at the start [were] his manuscripts, [showing] his opposition to the matters of Kabbalah, the fundamentals of which are known through select individuals of each generation prior to the RaMBa"N *z"l*, and afterwards through the RaMBa"N and the *Sefer HaBahir* and the *Zohar*. Now, his eminence did not add anything new with this opposition, except in the ferocity of its expression, **heretofore unseen among God-fearing Jews** (for one does not bring into the count those who

---

[86] Lit. 'the glory of his Torah' or 'the glory of the Torah of our master'

133

oppose this Kabbalah, who at the same time throw off
the revealed Torah, both written and oral).

Now, in matters of *halakha* there is a principle
brought by our teacher, Rab Moshe [Isserles, i.e. the
ReM"A] in *Shulḥan 'Arukh* (*Ḥoshen Mishpaṭ* 25:2 in the
name of the MoHaRI"Q), that 'anywhere that the words
of the earlier ones are written down, and they are well-
known, and [yet] the later legal decisors dispute them –
like how the decisors sometimes dispute the Geonim –
we go after the later legal decisors.' Since the claims [of
the earlier ones] have already been heard, and yet [the
later legal decisors] were not concerned for them, we
assume that they have found a correct reasoning not to
be concerned for them. Now, there is a claim against the
foundations of the Kabbalah regarding the matter of the
sefirot and the *aṣilut*, in that it appears as if, God forbid,
we are attributing multiplicity to the divine, which
would constitute the destruction of a foundation of the
law and a matter of idolatry, may God save us. But was
this not already discussed in the responsa of RIBa"SH
(157)? And his eminence should see the humility and fear
of respect with which [RIBa"SH] spoke, despite
distancing himself from the Kabbalah. For the disgrace
of suspecting multiplicity in the divine *sefirot*, he called
the contender who said 'the Christians believe in the
three-fold god, and the kabbalists believe in the ten-fold

god' by the title 'one of the philosophisers'[87] – clearly not respecting this opinion at all. Subsequently, [RIBa"SH] brought the explanation of Don Yosef b. Shushan, whom he respectfully calls 'the venerable sage,' [who explained] that the matter is similar to one who requests from the king that he grant him something through a certain emissary who is appointed over this. [RIBa"SH] wrote after [quoting] this explanation that 'behold, it is very good,'[88] and he was [ultimately] not concerned for a trace of idolatry, God forbid. The vast majority[89] of later authorities, who were holy and pure and eminent authorities of the world, accepted the words of the Kabbalah, despite having seen the claims of the contenders – the matter was therefore clear to them that there is no trace of idolatry, God forbid, in this matter, but rather an increasing in closeness to God and holiness. Now, were we to come and discuss the [kabbalistic]

---

[87] Heb. 'אחד המתפלספים', In Rav Kook's opinion, the verbal construction conveys a clearly cynical intention. It suggests someone who conducts themselves as if they were a philosopher, with quasi-intellectual arguments, but who is devoid of actual wisdom. However, it should be noted that this term is used frequently among medieval philosophical writers in a neutral sense.

[88] Gen. 1:31

[89] Heb. רובם ככולם. This is a piece of halakhic terminology, the meaning of which is that when the majority of a mixture of two substances is of one type, the minority of the other type can be ignored, and even subsumed into the majority. The implications of this terminology are immediately apparent.

expressions as they appear, without looking deeply into the matter; would this not be the same claim as [the claims of] corporealisation, [the expressions of which] are employed by the Torah, *Nebi'im* and *Ketubim*?[90] And according to RaMBa"M (*Hilkhot Teshuba* 3), is this [belief in a corporeal deity] not complete heresy, even if one says that there is indeed one Master, but that He has a body or image? Now, the RaABa"D excused these straying ones, because they were misled by the verses, and even more so by what they saw in the *aggadot* that confound people's minds. And so we must ask, why did the Torah and the *ḥakhamim* speak in this style, that risks confounding people? We must say that if there is a necessity to explain certain fundamental matters to understanding people or the masses, then the teacher will employ whatever terminology seems best to him, and he will rely on [other] *ḥakhamim* to come and clarify the matters and explain them to the fitting ones [who can understand the metaphor]. Thus the masses will continue to be directed through these matters to fear of heaven and good behaviour, and both types [i.e. the masses and the understanding people] will benefit. Now the RaMBa"M (*More Nebukhim* I:36) wrote that one who believes that God, may He be blessed, is physical or

---

[90] Rav Kook is referring to the many anthropomorphisms present in the *Tanakh*. These expressions cannot be taken at face value and must be understood metaphorically.

subject to [physical] actions is without doubt worse than one who worships idols. And yet, the Torah, the prophets and the *ḥakhamim* after them still chose to speak so freely in anthropomorphisms, and all the more so that there is no concern in homiletics to explain divine matters in purity of thought – [those divine matters] being utterly inarticulable – to explain them too in this style, that appears God forbid as multiplicitous, etc. And those who are capable of understanding the deeper [meaning of the] content will do so, and the simple person will tremble in fear, [understanding simply] that there is here a wondrous matter, and his fear of heaven will increase. As the author of *Ḥobot Halebabot* wrote in the second chapter of *Sha'ar HaYiḥud* in the name of the philosopher, that '[no one] can serve the most high, cause of all causes, save the prophet of the generation with his nature, or the expert philosopher with what he has acquired of wisdom.' Nonetheless, God's kindness is upon all his creations,[91] especially the Jewish people his close nation, and that [kindness] is that after accepting the unity of God, may He be blessed, through the Torah, then all the concepts, even those which are unclear, become clarified in the depths of their soul; such that ultimately they know that the truth in divine matters is far from the understanding of man, and after all the

---

[91] See *Olat ReIYa"H, Shaḥarit for Shabbat* 82

depictions, they fall back on [the position] that the matter is in accordance with how the holy Torah directs them.

Now, the foundations of *Kabbalah* were publicised in Yisrael through the fundamentals of the *sefirot* and *aṣilut* many generations before the publicising of the Zohar and its attribution to Rabbi Shimon bar Yoḥai – which, obviously, refers to its teachings and ways of understanding divinity, even if over the course of many generations there were different *ḥakhamim* who added to annotated it. And even if certain [questionable] things have crept in, that should be inspected – as his eminence, Rab Ya'aqob Emden did in his '*Miṭpaḥat*'[92] – the main [text of the Zohar] does not become nullified thus, as there are holy, lofty teachings wrapped in the cloak of *sod*, with deep terminology, all of which are intended [to show] the greatness of the actions of God, blessed be He, singular, individual and unique, blessed be He, Who has neither beginning nor end-purpose, and Whose understanding cannot be discerned. On

---

[92] Rav Kook himself advocated the position, first proposed by ḤID"A, that Emden only challenged the authenticity of the Zohar to weaken the position of the Sabbateans, who relied on statements therein to support their heresy. See *Oṣerot HaReIYa"H* II, 264, quoting Kook's commentary on *Ḥezyonei Amaṣiyahu*. In this letter, however, he does not suggest that as a line of argument, accepting the contents of *Miṭpaḥat Sefarim* at face value for the purposes of this argument.

similar matters Rabbi Shimon ben Laqish said: 'Many *pesuqim* that are fit to be burned are in fact the essence of Torah.'[93] The *ḥakhamim* were not concerned to discuss the *pasuq* 'Ascend to the Lord'[94] because of the question of the Sadducee, [which was] 'it should have said "Ascend to Me"', [and the *ḥakhamim* answered that] this is Metatron [speaking], whose name is the same as the name of his master.[95] Rashi comments there:[96] 'the Lord', i.e. Metatron is also called by the tetragrammaton, and [yet, the *ḥakhamim*] were not concerned at all that this would constitute multiplicity or an aspect of idolatry due to this being publicised and known, because all [such entities] are his servants and [divinely] influenced in their existence, and all their being is from Him, blessed be He; [the matter is] just that He apportioned to them of his honour and his abundant kindness, each one according to its level.

[97]In the *Midrash Rabba*[98] on the *pasuq* 'and he set up there an altar, *vayiqra lo el elohe yisrael*'[99], states: Said Resh

---

[93] *bḤollin* 60b

[94] Numbers 24:1. The speaker of this phrase is God Himself.

[95] *bSanhedrin* 38b

[96] Ibid. s.v. *shesh'mo*

[97] Rav Kook now provides further examples of mystical statements that are liable to be misinterpreted by the masses who cannot understand their nuance.

[98] *Bereshit Rabba, Vayyishlakh* 79:8.

[99] Genesis 33:20. Treating each set of words alone, this translates as 'and he called him' 'God' 'God of Israel'. The *Midrash* here engages

Laqish, '[Ya'aqob] said: "You are God in the upper realm, and I am god in the lower realm."' And in the *Yalqut* it is reversed: [Ya'aqob] said to Him: 'I am god in the upper realm and you in the lower realm,'[100] which is even more [explicit in its] mystical [exposition], and yet the *hakhamim* were not concerned that any smidgen of multiplicity or aspect of idolatry God forbid would come from this. Further, in the *gemara* in *Megilla*:[101] 'From where do we know that the holy One, blessed be He, called Ya'aqob '*el*'? As is said: "And he called him '*el*', the God of Israel" – who called him '*el*'? The God of Israel.

But why should we go looking for statements of the *hakhamim* in this regard? The Torah itself was unconcerned [to speak in this way]! The holy One, blessed be He said to Moshe Rabbenu, peace be upon him, 'and you will be to him as a god [Heb. *Elohim*]'[102], and 'I have set you as a god [Heb. *Elohim*] to Pharaoh'.[103] One who does not understand [these passages] could err with this, God forbid, and yet the Torah was not concerned, because of the ubiquitous knowledge that there is none other than He, blessed be He, and all these expressions are simply explanatory turns of phrase. And

---

with the syntactic ambiguity of the subject and direct/indirect object of the verb.

[100] *Yalqut Shimoni* 133:29.
[101] *bMegilla* 18a.
[102] *Exodus* 4:16
[103] Ibid. 7:1

this is not just the case with regarding to the shared name 'Elohim',[104] but it is even so with the essential name, which is not shared with any created thing, as I brought above regarding Metatron. In *Baba Batra* 78b[105]: In the future, the righteous shall be called by the name of God, as it says 'Anyone who is called in My name, and whom I have created for My honour, I have formed him, indeed made him.'[106] And it further says there: Three are called by the name of the holy One, blessed be He, and they are: the righteous, the messiah and Jerusalem. The righteous – as we have already said. The messiah, as it is written 'And this is his name, by which he shall be called: "The Lord [YHWH] is our righteousness".'[107] Jerusalem, as it is written 'Its perimeter will be eighteen thousand reeds, and the name of the city from that day will be "The Lord [YHWH] is there [Heb. *shama*]"[108] – do not read 'is there [*shama*]' but rather 'its name [*sh'maH*].' And RaSH"I[109] wrote: [this means] that their name will be the Lord.

---

[104] I.e., the word *Elohim* is polysemous and can refer to other entities besides God.

[105] The text reads 78b, this is presumably a printing error as the passage in question is located on 75b and the letter ח was mistakenly inserted for the letter ה.

[106] *Isaiah* 43:7

[107] *Jeremiah* 23:6

[108] *Ezekiel* 48:35

[109] This is in fact in the commentary of RaSHBa"M, RaSH"I's grandson. *bBaba Batra* ibid., s.v. *niqr'u 'al sh'mo*.

Someone who does not know, or does not believe in the sanctity of these things, could God forbid slander and defame through this, [saying] that there is here multiplicity in the divine, God forbid. And this is the same for the strange expressions found in Kabbalah. And so I do not understand what his eminence is criticising regarding the expressions that describe pairs, etc. – are these expressions more unbecoming than the physical actions? [Namely, as we see] in *Yoma* 54a: 'At the time that Israel would ascend for the pilgrimage, they would roll back the curtain [covering the ark], and show them the cherubim enveloped in each other, and would say to them "See [that] your desirousness before God is like the desirousness of a male and female".' And there they expounded upon the verse 'according to the space [Heb. *ma'ar*] of each [Heb. *ish*], and wreaths [Heb. *v'loyot*][110] to mean 'like a man [*ish*] who is embraced [*m'ore*] with his accompanier [*l'vaya*].[111] And RaSH"I explained, 'who is attached and embracing[112] his wife, between her arms.'[113] And certainly all of these are holy, pure depictions which stand far above any trace of impurity or [sexual] desire, God forbid, instead hinting to the sanctity of the Source of life, that all is contained within

---

[110] *I Kings* 7:36
[111] *bYoma* 54a–b
[112] Printed editions of RaSH"I read '*ḥabuq*', 'is embraced'.
[113] RaSH"I ibid.

His truth, may He be blessed, from start to finish – all of it is within his abode at the apex of purity and cleanliness; something that cannot be encapsulated in [articulable] idea. As RaMBa"M wrote:[114] 'All of existence, except the Creator, from the first formed creation until the tiny flea in the navel of the land, all derive existence from the strength of His truth. And because He knows Himself, and recognises His own greatness, splendour and truth, He knows everything, and nothing is hidden from Him.' If so, then the smallest of all creations, and naturally the smallest of all movements of living creatures – all derive existence from the strength of His truth, to the point where from the power of His Self-knowledge, blessed be He, He knows all of them, and thus there, in His supernal holiness, so to speak, is their ultimate existence at the apex of holiness and purity, with nothing unbecoming or [literal] imagery, God forbid. Such was the understanding of all the holy ones of Israel with their conception of the wisdom of Kabbalah and the foundations of the holy Zohar. In fact, were it not for this conception of holiness standing above any form of [literal] imagery, the terminology of the prophet would also be difficult: 'For as a young man would espouse a virgin, so shall your children espouse you.'[115] We would

---

[114] *Mishneh Torah, Hilkhot Yesode HaTorah* 2:9
[115] *Isaiah* 62:5. Text again mistakenly prints ח for ה.

143

have thought, God forbid, that this constitutes uncleanliness of expression! But from the side of sanctity, all are holy, and forfend ascribing to them slander or inappropriateness, be silent from even mentioning it! About this and similar matters they say in the *Mishna*:[116] 'The Song of Songs is holy of holies, and the entire world is not worthy as on the day the Song of Songs was given to Israel.'

Now the holy One blessed be He does not bring about misfortune through the righteous, God forbid, and 'the wholesomeness of the upright will lead them'[117] – all that is in regard to **general matters**, but with **specifics**, behold I say to his eminence as the *ḥaber* said to the *Kuzari* at the end of the third *ma'amar* (73): 'And I concede to you, king of Khazars, that there are matters in the *gemara* for which I am unable to give you a sufficient reason, nor bring them to any related matter.' And look at what he noted with regard to these matters, writing 'the composition will not lose out from discussing [only] the content I have mentioned.' So also not all the works that discussed Kabbalah are equal in their understanding and the manner of their speech, and there are works that are not accepted at all, such as '*Oz Le-lohim*', which his eminence brought, that if the

---

[116] *Yadayyim* 3:5
[117] *Proverbs* 11:3

author is [indeed] Naḥman[118] Ḥayyun – then he is known to tell over invalid [statements] of the followers of the false messiah Shabbetai Ṣebi. Or perhaps you have in your possession [another] book of this name, of a different matter, for which we cannot be held accountable. Additionally, the people who have not reached an inner understanding, should set their activity in what befits them and their intellectual capabilities – [namely] the simple understanding of the holy Torah; how good their portion is! But **forfend to ally [yourself] with those who change things**, and to slander this holy wisdom in its entirety, which the majority of the great and holy ones of Israel all venerate and sanctify it wholeheartedly and in holy and pure faith – if only our portion should be among them!

His eminence should see in *Eṣ Ḥayyim*[119] where he discusses the matter of *ṣimṣum*, the understanding of which is at the highest level [of understanding], and in that place[120] there is a small note of the eminent Rabbi Meir [Ashlag], author of the *panim me'irot [umasbirot]* z"l, who wrote: 'Meir said: the *Rab* said this **from our perspective**.' From here we know that all these matters are said from our perspective – that is, according to the

---

[118] This appears to be erroneous, as his name is recorded as Neḥemiah.

[119] *Hekhal, Sha'ar Rish'on, 'anaf* 2.

[120] S.v. *veda'*

145

intellectual capacity of created entities, in the purest, loftiest way. In truth, this is the praise and greatness of the supreme king of kings, the holy One blessed be He: that in order to explain the extreme edge of the greatness of his actions, particularly the spiritual, intellectual and moral ones that are much more wondrous than the physical and natural ones, incredible depth and explanations using very deep language are required; to the extent that it is valid to employ allegorical depictions in order to cling to Him, may His name be blessed, in love, fear, and pure and holy clinging. Now certainly, from the perspective of His essence, may His name be blessed, were it not for His desire and His will in His worlds and among His creations and those who do His will, it would be completely impossible to devise any form of parable or attach any idea to Him – indeed, this is what they intend in general with the worlds of *En-Sof*. But from the perspective of His will that is dedicated to renewing creation with no end, and to guiding those with intelligence and free will along the upright path according to the light of life – on this plane come all the parables whose light is revealed to the remnant whom God calls, each man according to his level. And the difference between the secret content of Kabbalah and the purity of the upright, simple intellect is not so great for those who know understanding, who direct their hearts to the heavens truly and wholesomely.

My hope is strong, with the help of God, may He be blessed, that his eminence will penetrate into my words and return[121] and say: 'Surely the Lord is in this place',[122] [this place] of the light of the hidden wisdom of Israel in its sanctity, just as the vast majority[123] of the ḥakhamim of Israel accepted and upheld upon themselves.[124] And 'The secret of the Lord [He makes known] to those who fear Him, and His covenant to make known to them,'[125] **and for all that his eminence spoke against them we shall judge him favourably, for his intention was for the sake of heaven, and may the Lord forgive him,**[126] and may it be fulfilled in his eminence [the *pasuq*] 'May those who fear You return to me, and those who know Your testimonies.'[127]

---

[121] Or: repent. In a letter not referring to Mori Qafiḥ by name but directed against him, Rav Kook wrote that one who besmirches the holy books of *kabbalah*, and the rabbis who study it, is subject to the same punishment given one who speaks badly about Torah scholars. See *Iggerot HaReIYa"H* II, no. 626.

[122] *Genesis* 28:16. This could also imply a suggested further admission of ignorance on Mori Qafiḥ's part, as the *pasuq* continues 'but I did not know.'

[123] See n.5 above.

[124] *Megillat Esther* 9:27

[125] *Psalms* 25:14

[126] Paraphrasing e.g., *Numbers* 30:6

[127] *Psalms* 119:79

And may the honour of his magnanimous soul be at peace, and the soul of his dear friend blesses him from the holy [place] in the holy land.

Abraham Yitzhak HaKohen Kook

Letter 2

Rabbi Qafiḥ responds to Rabbi Kook

Date: 15ᵗʰ Iyyar 5691 [28ᵗʰ August 1931]

To the honourable great Rabbi, master of his people and leader of his nation,[128] the *kohen* our teacher Rabbi Abraham Yitzḥak HaKohen Kook, may God protect him, 'For the lips of the priest shall preserve knowledge and they will seek Torah from his mouth, for he is an angel of the Lord of hosts.'[129] I received your letter, our master, dated 26ᵗʰ *Ṭebet* close to Pesaḥ, 'You are the anointed cherub, covering'[130] sound counsel with the wings of his understanding[131] to straighten the crooked and perverse,[132] like the pillar of fire and cloud before the

---

[128] *bKetubot 17a*

[129] *Malakhi 2:7*

[130] *Ezekiel 28:14*

[131] The same poetic hyperbole to introduce the respondent at the start of a letter can be found in *Teshubot HaRIBa"SH* #229.

[132] Vid. *Isaiah* 42:16 and 45:2. The direct quote is probably lifted from *Mishne Torah, Hilkhot Sheḥita* 14:16, although all bar one (T–S

149

Israelite camp, with *pilpul* and sharpness to find favour and sound intellect in the eyes[133] of all, like a scholar of the Rabbis whom the residents of his town are fond of![134]

However, our master and teacher, you should know that it behoves every sharp and acute[135] individual to guard the way to the tree of life,[136] lest in his *pilpul* he dilute the Torah, leaving the truth wanting. For every drive and desire of one who fears the word of God [should be] to stand the truth upon its establishment, as many of the *hakhamim* spoke about at length, including the *kohen* our teacher Rabbi Natan Adler, in his general introduction to his commentary of *Targum Onkelos*.[137]

AS 95.158) of discovered early manuscripts in fact read המעשים for המעקשים.

[133] *Proverbs* 3:4

[134] *bKetubot* 105b, preserving an earlier, more accurate textual variant. There may be a subtle implication that Rav Kook is adopting an untrue position in order to keep people happy, as the context of this passage is a Torah scholar who is beloved because he does not rebuke those living in his town.

[135] The Hebrew denotes someone competent at *pilpul*.

[136] *Genesis* 3:24. This alludes to the appellation of 'cherub' above, as the '*kerubim*' were stationed east of the Garden of Eden to 'guard the way to the tree of life'.

[137] Chief Rabbi Nathan Adler of Britain, who composed a commentary on *Onkelos* entitled *Netina LaGer*. I am unsure as to why Mori Qafih would single out this example of all people. Perhaps, during Rav Kook's time in London, he became acquainted with Rabbi Adler's son, Hermann Adler, Chief Rabbi at the time? This does not seem convincing though.

Now, what his esteemed eminence brought from the words of Qolon [i.e. the MoHaRI"Q] (brought in the notes of the ReM"A 25:2) – there is no proof from there at all, for these words apply to [the principle of] the *halakha* following the most recent opinion[138] when it is **against a particular *gaon***, but not against a ***tanna*** or an ***amora***, as is written there. Meaning, from Abbaye and Raba onwards, and [only] if one brings a proof for his words, as the RaMBa"M did in his composition, where he [would] bring a proof for his words against a *gaon*. But without this, anything stated in the words of a *gaon* – we hearken to [that *gaon*], as Rabbenu Tam wrote in many places.

And what his esteemed eminence brought from the words of the RIBa"SH (157) – on the contrary! From there is a proof in the opposite direction, for there he wrote that Rabbi Pereṣ HaKohen would not discuss nor ascribe {divinity} to those *sefirot*, and he also heard from his mouth that Rabbi Shimshọn of Qinon – who was a Rabbi greater than all of his contemporaries, and who [RIBa"SH] also recalled hearing [directly] from him, – [Rabbi Pereṣ] said: "'I pray [with the simplicity of] the mind of a child," that is to say he excludes himself from the kabbalists [who pray to different *sefirot*].' And regarding what he wrote, that 'I have already heard one

---

[138] Known as *hilkheta kebatra'ei*.

of the philosophisers etc.', the *Bet Yehuda* has already written that these [words of the philosopher] are the words of RiBa"SH himself, and he ascribed the opinion to 'one of the philosophisers' because he was afraid lest the pursuers attack him! [*Bet Yehuda*] further wrote there: 'Is there indeed divinity to the *sefirot*, such that one should pray to them? We see that it is obvious to [RIBa"SH] that there is no divinity, such that one should pray to them!'

The explanation of Don Yosef b. Shushan does not relate to the words of the Zohar or the *mequbalim* at all, it is simply **evading the question**, for all the *mequbalim* who are drawn after the Zohar say that the 'Ze'ir Anpin is our god, and we are his people and servants', as *Sefer HaBerit* wrote (*ma'amar* 20:15), and *Yosher Lebab* (page 4), and that [*Ze'ir Anpin*] is the one who brought us out of Egypt, and his wife *Malkhut* is the one who struck the Egyptians in Egypt and by the sea, and he was the one who was revealed to our ancestors at Mount Sinai and gave us the Torah, as the author of *Naḥalat Yosef* wrote, and that all *korbanot* that Israel would offer up and all *tefillot* and *berakhot* without exception are for the sake of *Ze'ir Anpin*, who is our god! And because RIBa"SH understood that the words of our master, Rabbi Yosef Shushan were not correct, he therefore distanced himself from this *Kabbalah*! How can an Israelite, who believes in the holy words of the written and oral Torah, believe that the verse 'Know the God of your fathers, and serve Him'[139] refers to the five *parṣufim* and serving the *Ze'ir Anpin* – **despite its being created, for you are serving its soul** (as is written in *Yosher Lebab* and *Sefer HaBerit*)!

And with regard to what his eminence said, that 'Were we to come and discuss the [kabbalistic] expressions as they appear [without looking deeply into the matter; would this not be the same claim as [the claims of] corporealisation, [the expressions of which] are employed by the Torah, *Nebi'im* and *Ketubim*?]' – we are not discussing the expressions but rather the actual [kabbalistic] faith that stands in contradiction to the faith of the holy Torah![140] Now when the Torah

---

[139] *I Chronicles* 28:9

[140] This sentence is key to understanding a major part of the (ongoing) dispute between those who attack the *kabbalah* and those who seek to defend it. Reading between the lines of Rav Kook's letter, it emerges that he does not believe Mori Qafiḥ correctly understood the kabbalistic concepts. (Rav Kook explicitly writes this in a letter written five years earlier, later published as an approbation for *'Emunat Hashem*, a book written to respond to the arguments of Qafiḥ's *Milḥamot Hashem*; see *Mo'adei HaReIYa"H* pp. 441-442.) According to Kook, the kabbalistic ideas are deep, lofty matters, and taking them at face value is a mistake. Once this is understood, the theological issues of *kabbalah* simply fall away. As seen in Kook's letter, we know that these expressions are not to be taken literally, because such great rabbis as Meir Ashlag have told us not to. In other words, the later kabbalists can and do accurately represent the original intent of the *Zohar*. Although certain ideas or phrases in early *kabbalah* may initially appear misleading, the later kabbalists

153

and all the prophets and our *ḥakhamim* utilised physical descriptions [such as] 'the hand of God', 'the eyes of God', 'the ears of God', that was only out of necessity that requires us to describe His existence and make Him known through terms with which people are familiar, [such as when] informing children, women and the masses. This necessity brought us to corporealise the Creator, may He be blessed, and to tell [His aspects] over

---

clarified what is meant by these ideas, and thus rendered them acceptable. This insistence on the absolute homogeneity of the *kabbalah* is an undeniable tenet of the defence of the authenticity of the *kabbalah*. For example, a recent translator of Joseph Ergas' *Shomer Emunim* wrote as follows:

> From an inspection of the underlying Kabbalistic concepts that are laid out very clearly in Shomer Emunim, it should be blatantly obvious that R. Qafich [sic.] lacked any proper understanding, knowledge and context of the basic Kabbalistic concepts that he claimed were blasphemous.

Since Ergas is the true, faithful representative of Lurianic *kabbalah*, and AR"I the true, faithful representative of the *Zohar*, any attack on the *Zohar* must take into account its reinterpretation in later *kabbalah*. (That such a view is untenable can be seen from even a cursory review of the relevant chapters in Scholem's *Major Trends in Jewish Mysticism*.) Thus, although Qafiḥ is not addressing the *Shomer 'Emunim*, this line of argumentation by the above translator pits Qafiḥ's position against his 'authoritative' explanation of the seemingly heretical passages of the *Zohar*. Mori Qafiḥ thus introduces the following sections of his response by pointing out that he is not talking about semantics and 'expressions', but rather the obvious corporealisations and divine multiplicity that underpins these expressions – dispensing with the idea that the later revisionism of these passages is in fact the true representation of their intent.

in terms of created beings, in order that [the concept of] His existence, may He be blessed, should enter into their souls via words that are closer to their intellect and understanding. Were they to relate [God] in the fitting manner, using spiritual terminology, [the masses] would understand neither the matter nor even the words. Therefore, the terminology needs – at first – to be physically descriptive, and [only] after that we inform them the truth of the matter of these idioms. [This is] as the holy Torah itself did, where it spoke at first with physical expressions [such as] 'and I will send my hand'[141], 'and I will pass through the land of Egypt'[142], and after that exceedingly gave warning, saying 'And you will carefully guard yourselves [not to make a graven image,] for you saw no image [of God]'[143]. And thus did our prophets: they employed physical terminology, but then warned in God's name, saying 'But to whom shall you liken Me, that I shall be equal? Or [to whom] will you compare me, that I shall be like [that]?'[144] 'And to whom shall you liken God? And as

---

[141] *Exodus* 3:20

[142] Ibid. 12:12

[143] *Deuteronomy* 4:15

[144] This appears to be a misquote. The intended text is from Isaiah 46:5, which begins למי תדמיוני, and not ואל מי תדמיוני, which appears (without the second clause quoted here) in Isaiah 40:25.

what likeness shall you value Him?'[145] But to depict within His unity multiple faces? Be silent from mentioning [such a thing]!

The Talmud states in Sanhedrin: 'After the death of the latter prophets Ḥaggai, Zekharia and Malʾakhi, the *ruaḥ haqodesh* departed from Israel; however, they would still utilise a *bat qol*.'[146] And Rabbi Shimʿon b. Yoḥai himself, as well as his son Rabbi Elʿazar, received a *bat qol* [saying] 'Exit your cave', as is brought in *Shabbat*.[147] And in *Meʿila*, when the *ḥakhamim* sent RaSHB"Y and Rabbi Elʿazar b. Rabbi Yose to appease [the emperor] in order to annul the decree that the ruling power had decreed, [namely] that [the Jews] not circumcise their sons, nor observe Shabbat, and that they have relations with their wives whilst impure from menstruation, and b. Temalion[148] said to them:

'Do you wish for me to join you?' RaSHB"Y cried and said: 'A *malʾakh* happened upon the

---

[145] Ibid. 40:18. This quote may be chosen pointedly, as it is used in the Zohar quoted shortly after to refer instead to the supremacy of the *adam qadmon*.

[146] *bSanhedrin* 11a. This also appears in *bYoma* 9b and *Soṭa* 48b.

[147] *bShabbat* 33b

[148] In all Rabbinic literature, this name is identified with a cunning (human) deceiver, see e.g. *Vayyiqra Rabba* 6:3. Later Ashkenazi writers such as RaSH"I (s.v. *ben Temalion*) identify this with a demon, and the Tosafot (s.v. *yaṣa liqrato*) with a type of elf (or *lutin*) common in French folklore.

maidservant of my father's house[149] three times, but [for] me not [even] once! But nonetheless, let the miracle come.' [Ben Temalion] went ahead to the daughter of the Caesar, when [RaSHB"Y] arrived there he said 'Out, ben Temalion!' and once he called to him, he left and went [on his way].

Thus we see that RaSHB"Y did not merit prophecy, even through a *mal'akh*! Yet in the Zohar,[150] it states that the holy One, blessed be He, Who is called the *atiq yomin*, was revealed to RaSHB"Y in his study hall (as the *Miqdash Melekh* wrote,[151] that RaSHB"Y was certain that this [entity that] was revealed was the *atiq [yomin]* and not the *arikh [anpin]*, even though both are called *sabba d'sabbin*[152]). [*Atiq yomin*] revealed to [RaSHB"Y] things which are forbidden to hear! [Namely,] that the Creator, who is *abba*, who would say to *imma* 'it should be so,' and

---

[149] I.e., Hagar, maidservant of Abraham.

[150] See Zohar I, 22a-b.

[151] Ad loc.

[152] *Sabba d'sabbin* refers to the *sefira* of *keter*, which sits above the *sabbin* of *ḥokhma ubina*. The *atiq yomin* and *arikh anpin* are the two *parṣufim* of *keter*, the former representing inner motivation and the latter outward divine will. *Miqdash Melekh* is arguing that RaSHB"Y was certain that this came from the inner motivation and not from the outward divine will, despite them both being configurations of the same *sefira*.

she would do so immediately;[153] he would say 'let there be light,' and 'let there be firmament,' and 'let the waters gather,' and 'let there be luminaries,' and she would do so immediately. But the statement 'let us make man' – the *imma* said to *abba*: 'Let us make man,' for 'let us' surely refers to two [entities]. But *abba* did not want to join in [man's] creation, for his end would be to sin, thus *imma* created *Adam HaRishon* against *abba*'s will, [such that] even though he is *ben kesil*,[154] he remains the sorrow of his mother[155] and not the sorrow of his father. But, the supernal man (*ze'ir* [*anpin*]) is in the way of *aṣilut* – he is the *ben ḥakham*[156] who is a son to both *abba* and *imma*. And therefore, when *Adam HaRishon* sinned with the tree of knowledge, he was driven out of the Garden of Eden and [*imma*] was driven out with him. And it further explains there that the divinity that said 'See now that I Myself am He, and there is no god with Me,'[157] was [in fact] the *adam qadmon*, who is above all the *parṣufim*, who need not gain permission from anyone above him!

Is this not false prophecy?! For RaSHB"Y cried that he had not happened upon a *mal'akh* even once, and

---

[153] The following examples are all to be found in *Genesis* 1.

[154] Lit. 'the son of the fool.' The paradigmatic *adam* of *qelipa* is called '*kesil*', thus when a human being succumbs to this *kesil* and sins, he is called *ben kesil*.

[155] Heb. '*tugat immo*' (*Proverbs* 10:1).

[156] In contrast to the *ben kesil*, see ibid.

[157] *Deuteronomy* 32:39

[yet] in the Zohar he said that the holy One, blessed be He, Who is called *atiq*, was revealed to him, and not in a dream but awake, within the study hall, calling out to him 'Shimọn, Shimọn etc.' – is this not belief in multiple authorities in heaven?

Now Pesaḥim states:

> 'And Ya'aqob called to his sons, and said "Be gathered, that I may tell you [that which will happen at the end of days]".'[158] Ya'aqob sought to reveal the end of days to his sons, and the *shekhina* departed from him. He said: 'Perhaps, God forbid, there is in my offspring something unfit, like Abraham from whom came Yishmaẹl, and my father Yiṣḥaq from whom came Esav?' His sons said to him: 'Hear, O Israel, the Lord is our God, the Lord is One.'[159] They said: 'Just as there is only one [God] in your heart, so too there is only one [God] in our heart.' At that moment, Ya'aqob our father opened and said: 'Blessed be the name of the glory of His kingdom, forever.'[160]

---

[158] *Genesis* 49:1
[159] *Deuteronomy* 6:4
[160] *bPesaḥim* 56a

But in the Zohar:[161]

> 'Hear, O Israel' – Said Rabbi Yesa: [This refers to] *Yisrael Sabba*.[162] Said Rabbi Yiṣḥaq: The large letter *'ayin* [in the writing of the *shema*] incorporates the seventy names that bear witness to everything {the *sod* of *bina* which has within it seventy names}, 'Hear, O Israel' as is written 'Hear, O heavens'[163] and 'Give ear, O heavens'[164] – so too here, 'Hear, O Israel' {*zeir*}, and all of this is one idea.
>
> 'YHWH' – the head of everything, illuminated from the *'atiqa qadisha*, which is called *ab* {*abba* receives from *arikh*}.
> 'Our God' – the depth of streams and fountains [whence it] comes and is drawn to all {*imma*}.
> 'YHWH' – the body of the tree, the completeness of the roots {*zeir*}.
> 'One' – the congregation of Israel {*malkhut*}!

Behold it is explicitly explained that in saying '*Shema Yisrael, YHWH E-lohenu YHWH eḥad*,' it included

---

[161] Zohar III, 263a

[162] The explanation of *Yisrael Sabba* is beyond the scope of a footnote.

[163] *Isaiah* 1:2

[164] *Deuteronomy* 32:1

within it **five separate *parṣufim***, and one joins them
and ties them with his intention, [for them] to be one!
Tell us, our master, teacher, Rabbi – what 'additional
closeness to God and holiness' is there with this?! On the
contrary, it imitates the Christians who believe in the
Trinity, as the RIBa"SH wrote in the name of one of the
Torah philosophers. (See the commentary of Rabbi
Ọbadia S'forno, *Deuteronomy* 13:3, 17:3 and 21:14, and
his commentary to *Psalms* 16.)

Now it is clear that all the masses of the people of
Israel and their *ḥakhamim* who were occupied in *Talmud
Babli* and *Yerushalmi*, and *Midrash Rabba* and *Tanḥuma*
and similar true *midrashim* of our Rabbis *z"l* – their
earnest intention was to serve HaShem, as Rabbi
Shimshọn of Qinon said [regarding conception of God]:
'I pray for the mind of this child, who has nothing in his
heart save unity, without the partnership of any aspect,
but simply [desires] to crown [God] as king in heaven
and earth'; as our Rabbis *z"l* said, without partnership
with any other thing. As RaSHB"Y the *tanna*[165] said:
'Anyone who unites the name of heaven with something
else, is removed from the world, as it says: "One who

---

[165] This adjective is charged, suggesting that this statement was said
by the **real** RaSHB"Y, i.e., the *tanna*, as opposed to other
pseudepigraphic statements. See also below p.13.

sacrifices to a god shall be banned, [sacrifice] only to the Lord alone"[166].[167]

It is a great wonder, and large mystery, why his esteemed eminence saw [fit] to bring here *derashot* of our rabbis, *z"l*, on the verse 'and he set up there an altar, *vayiqra lo el elohe yisrael*' – 'Said Resh Laqish: I am God in the upper realms and you are god in the lower realms, etc.'. Because Ya'aqob [deigned to] call himself *'el'*, God became angry with him for taking greatness and authority for himself, as Rab Huna explains in the name of Resh Laqish: '[God] said to him: Not even the sexton of the synagogue does not rise to the Torah scroll until called; by your life! Tomorrow your daughter will go out [and be raped].'[168] (See RaSH"I's commentary and *Yefe Toar* [ad loc.].) And [considering] the words of the Gemara [in which] said Rabbi Aḥa quoting Rabbi El'azar that the holy One, blessed be He called Ya'aqob *'el'*, unlike [the statement of] Resh Laqish! It is obvious that all these expressions are only expressions of greatness, authority and power; similarly, 'I have set you as a god [Heb. *Elohim*] to Pharaoh'[169] [and] 'and you will be to him as a god [Heb. *Elohim*]'[170], and 'In the future, the

---

[166] *Exodus* 22:19

[167] *bSanhedrin* 63a

[168] This is a variation of the text found in *Bereshit Rabba* and *Yalquṭ Shimoni* op. cit.

[169] *Exodus* 7:1

[170] Ibid. 4:16

righteous shall be called by the name of God,' as well as the Messiah and Jerusalem.[171] Which fool thinks that all these *derashot* [connote] multiplicity in the divine?! Is it sensible to say concerning Ya'aqob our father 'you are our God' and that we should pray to him? Does it not already say: 'Though Abraham not know us, and Yisrael not recognise us – You are the Lord'[172]? And similarly, Aharon – how would it be possible for him to say to Moshe 'you are my God' and serve him and pray to him? Rather certainly all of [these examples] are expressing importance and greatness, in the same way as judges are called '*elohim*': 'To the judges shall come the matter of the two of them,'[173] 'Judges shall you not curse,'[174] [and] 'And the sons of *Elohim* saw'[175] [which] the Targum [renders] 'princes'[176].[177]

I have already informed you, our master and teacher, that we are not discussing the expression but rather the fundamental faith to serve created powers, as I explained in *Milḥamot HaShem* and in the pamphlet *Da'at E-lohim*, and nothing his esteemed eminence has brought bears even the scent of proof [against me] at all!

---

[171] *bBaba Batra* 75b

[172] *Isaiah* 63:16

[173] *Exodus* 22:8

[174] Ibid. v.27

[175] *Genesis* 6:2

[176] *TgO* ad loc.

[177] See also *More Nebukhim* I:2

Even that which his esteemed eminence brought from what our rabbis, *z"l*, said in *Yoma*, 'At the time that Israel would ascend for the pilgrimage, they would roll back the curtain [covering the ark], and show them the cherubim enveloped in each other, and would say to them "See [that] your desirousness before God is like the desirousness of a male and female",' as expounded [from] 'according to the space of each, and wreaths'[178] – 'like a man who is embraced with his accompanier'.[179] The meaning is that the cherubim were touching each other as loving partners who go hand in hand, for it is impossible to say that the spreading of their wings changed such that they held each other [directly], for it is written 'and the cherubim shall be of spread wings above'[180] – 'and they shall be,' i.e. as they are, so shall they remain,[181] and it is explained in the *pesuqim* that they were fixed at two ends of the [ark] cover, thus it is impossible that they would draw close to each other and touch each other! And so too the wings of the cherubim that Shelomo made were touching each other one wing to the second, and both wings were pointing inwards

---

[178] *I Kings* 7:36

[179] *bYoma* loc. cit.

[180] *Exodus* 25:20

[181] This *derasha* is used by the *ḥakhamim* to require something to remain unchanged, utilising the 'superfluous' copula היה to convey an added existential element to its subject. See, for example, *bBerakhot* 13a, *bMegilla* 9a.

[towards] the other's wings. And this is what our rabbis, *z"l*, said '*m'orim*' with each other – not that they left their place and their bodies were suspended miraculously and they then came to embrace one another, for this was not the case and did not occur! Rather, [they were] as partners who go hand in hand!

Now if it is as you say, our master and teacher, that these *parṣufim* are depictions of holiness and purity, then what place is there to attribute to them limbs of sexual intercourse, [as in] 'the *yesod*[182] of the male and *yesod* of the female'?! Since they are created and are acted upon by the force above them, **they cannot be the source of life**, as his esteemed eminence thought, for only our God who created us – He alone is the source of life, as it says: 'They have forsaken me, the source of the waters of life.'[183]

With regard to what his esteemed eminence wrote, [that] 'were it not for this conception of holiness [standing above any form of literal imagery],' then the particular idiom of the *pasuq* would have been difficult, [in that it says]: 'For as a young man would espouse a virgin, so shall your children espouse you'[184] – it is a great wonder how a mouth as holy as yours, our master and teacher, could say such a thing. For it is obvious that in

---

[182] *Yesod* is the *sefira* affiliated with the reproductive organs.

[183] *Jeremiah* 2:13.

[184] *Isaiah* 62:5

all the holy writings the noun '*ba'al*' means **the master of something that is acquired to it**, [as in] '*ba'al* of the ox', '*ba'al* of a pit', '*ba'al* of a woman.' And the meaning of the *pasuq* 'For as a young man would espouse a virgin' [is] just as a man **acquires** a woman, so shall the land **be acquired** to them in order to settle it in peace and tranquillity, 'with none to make [them] afraid'[185], as Yonatan b. Uzziel translated, 'As a young man dwells with a virgin, so shall your sons dwell with you.'[186] And HaRaMBa"M *z"l* wrote in the *Guide* that in *leshon haqodesh* there are no direct words for marital relations, but instead [all such matters are referred to] by way of analogy: he will have mastery over, he will lie, he will take, he will uncover nakedness – as our rabbis *z"l* said: 'A person should never utter an unseemly thing from his lips, for behold the *pasuq* spoke around the subject etc.'[187]

Forfend to compare the idioms of the holy book *Song of Songs* – the most praised and excellent of all songs, which discusses the desirousness of Israel before the holy One, blessed be He, as our rabbis *z"l* said: 'A parable to a king who had one daughter, and he loved her exceedingly; he did not move from his love of her

---

[185] See e.g., *Jeremiah* 46:27.

[186] *TgY* ad loc.

[187] *bPesahim* 3a (the text mistakenly prints 13). This refers to the Torah's choice to use additional words instead of concise brevity to express something not as 'unclean' but rather as 'not clean'.

until he called her "my sister", as it says "open for me, my sister"[188]; nor did he move from his love of her until he called her "my mother", as it says "listen to me my people and nation [Heb. *leumi*]"[189] {[for] *'le'imi'* ['to my mother'] is written}; nor did he move from his love of her until he called her "my daughter", as it says "hear, my daughter, and see"[190].[191] And so it is with the desirousness of Israel for the holy One, blessed be He, as it says: 'My beloved is to me, and I am to him' – He is to me as a God, and I am to Him as a nation, He is to me as a father, and I {will be} to Him as a son, [He is to me] as a shepherd, and I am to Him as a flock, He is to me as a watchman, and I am to Him as a vineyard, etc.'[192] –

His esteemed eminence, our master, erred in comparing the idioms of the words of the living God [in] *Song of Songs* to this foreign book **which disgraces the word of HaShem, the Mishnah and Talmud** (*Zohar Bereshit* 27 and in *Parashat Teṣe* p.179, and in many places in the *Zohar* and *Tiqqunim*), in that the one and unique God, who has no form of body, joins together and ties the god whom the 'male' and 'female' serve (i.e., *ze'ir* and his *nuqba*), like his statement: 'And you are he who joins

---

[188] *Song of Songs* 5:2.
[189] *Isaiah* 51:4
[190] *Psalms* 45:11
[191] *Shemot Rabba* 52:5
[192] *Shir HaShirim Rabba* 2:16

together the holy One, blessed be He, and His *shekhina*.'[193]

And regarding what the master brought from Resh Laqish, who said: 'Many *pesuqim* that are fitting to be burned are in fact the essence of Torah,'[194] RaSH"I *z"l* explains: 'Many *pesuqim* seem to those who read them as fitting to be burned – that He should not have written them, for they are not needed in the Torah, and it is a disgrace to join them with sanctity.'[195] This means to say, not that there are in [these *pesuqim*] statements that appear like heresy, God forbid, like [in] the *Zohar* that the *hakhamim* of Toledo received from the servants of an idolatrous king, one of the kings of the east, as the Rabbi HID"A wrote in *Shem HaGedolim, Ma'arekhet Sefarim,* letter *zayin*.[196]

Now I have already indicated to his esteemed eminence the places where the Zohar ascribes the *aboda* to the short face (*ze'ir anpin*), and it is explained and agreed upon by the *mequbbalim*, as is explained in *Sefer HaBerit* 20:15, in the name of *Yosher Lebab*, and he [speaks] at length there with many proofs from the Zohar and the *Tiqqunim* that the *aboda* [is performed] for

---

[193] *Zohar* III, 109b.

[194] *bHollin* 60b

[195] RaSH"I ad loc.

[196] This refers to HID"A's description of the discovery of the Zohar, reported in *Shem HaGedolim*.

the *ze'ir anpin*. Thus wrote the AR"I in *Liqqute Tanakh* on the *pasuq* 'Trust in the Lord forever,'[197] and thus wrote Rab Ḥayyim Viṭal in *Eṣ Ḥayyim, Sha'ar HaKelalim* 11, that Moshe Rabbenu *a"h* said to Yisrael when they entered the land that the Lord your God is the *ze'ir* and his *nuqba*. And so too in *Maḥberet HaQodesh* in *Seder Musaf Shabbat*, he wrote that the angels, the masses on high, give a crown to *ze'ir anpin*, who is the Lord our God, and thus wrote *Meṣaref HaEmuna* at the end. Also, in *Miqdash Melekh* (p.12) s.v. *'Elaha Rabreba'* [= great God] he wrote that this [refers to] *ze'ir anpin*, and one who directs his *tefilla* to the *En Sof* – his *tefilla* is not valid; and thus wrote *Naḥalat Yosef*. And as it is explained in the Zohar, that the *ze'ir anpin* was created, and is the *adam* of *aṣilut*, who is called 'the wise son [who] delights the father,'[198] and dominion is granted to him over all things, and all things should worship him, and anyone who withholds a blessing from this son will have his sins presented before the *imma qadisha*, the mother herself.[199]

It is explained explicitly that the *'aboda* and all blessings [are directed] towards *ze'ir anpin*, who receives his kingship from what is above him, and not [directed] towards our God, who said 'I am the first and I am the

---

[197] *Isaiah* 26:4

[198] *Proverbs* 10:1

[199] *Zohar* III, 192a

last,'[200] about which our rabbis *z"l* explained, 'He did not receive his kingship from another, nor will he give it over to another, and besides him there is no God – in that he has no partner.'[201] This is not so with these *parṣufim* who are called *illot* 'that not a single one of these *illot* can take a single action until it has received permission from the one above it,' as we explained above regarding 'let us make man', that '**let us** necessarily refers to two, as this one said to the one above it '**let us** [make man]', but could not do anything without permission and instruction from the one above it; and [in turn] the one above it cannot do anything until it takes advice from its neighbour [above it], etc.'[202] Do these words not constitute belief in multiple authorities? Is there not, in serving the little face (*ze'ir anpin*), the serving of a foreign god? Is there not in their[203] saying **that you serve [*ze'ir anpin*]'s soul** the uniting of the name of heaven with something else? And the true *tanna* RaSHB"Y said: 'Anyone who unites the name of heaven with something else, is removed from the world, as it says: "One who sacrifices to a god shall be banned, [sacrifice] only to the Lord alone"[204]!'[205] Is this belief not similar to the belief of

---

[200] *Isaiah* 44:6

[201] See *Shir HaShirim Rabba* 1:9 and *ySanhedrin* 2a.

[202] *Zohar* I, 22b.

[203] See supra *Yosher Leibab* and *Sefer HaBerit*.

[204] *Exodus* 22:19.

[205] *bSanhedrin* 63a.

the nations of the world, who 'from Tyre and westward, and from Carthage and eastward, they call {the God of Israel} the God of the gods,'[206] but they ascribe power and dominion to those divine powers that are under him.[207]

The *ḥakhamim z"l* already gave over to us a great principle in belief: Everything has derivatives [lit. generations]: 'The heavens and earth have derivatives etc. … It was taught: [Anything that has derivatives dies and becomes worn out, and is created and does not create. And] anything that has no derivatives[208] neither dies nor becomes worn out, and creates and is not created. Rabbi 'Azariah b. Rabbi said: This refers to [the One] above.'[209] And the Rabbi [of] *Eṣ Yosef* explained:[210] 'Dies and becomes worn out' – wearing out [refers to] whilst it is still alive, for all existing beings would continually lack more and more were it not for the holy One, blessed be He renewing each day constantly the act of creation, and 'death' [refers to] loss. 'And whatever has no derivatives' {meaning there is no [external] reason for its existence} – even though this refers only to the holy One, blessed be He, on account of the first clause

---

[206] *bMenaḥot* 110a.

[207] See RaSH"I and MaHaRSH"A ad loc.

[208] The text in the printed letter reads 'that has derivatives', which appears to be a misprint from the previous line of the *midrash*.

[209] *Bereshit Rabba* 12:7, *Yalquṭ Shimoni* 18:1.

[210] Ad loc.

teaching 'anything', the latter clause [also] taught
'anything'. [This is] as Rabbi 'Azariah b. Rabbi
explained, [that] 'this refers to [the One] above.' And
thus wrote Rabbi Ḥoter ben Shelomo[211] in explaining
the fourth foundation of the thirteen foundations that
HaRaMBa"M *z"l* wrote: 'He is the First Being, who has
no start, nor any other existing being besides Him. And
the renewing is of what He created and caused to be
besides Him.' Since these *sefirot* and *parṣufim* have above
them an *illa* that gives them existence, they are created
beings and not creators. But the name of the holy One,
blessed be He, which is common in the *midrashim* of the
rabbis *z"l* and in the mouth of every person of Israel, is
only rightfully used [to refer to] our God, **the first
cause**, and also to the unique names – even if [others]
are called by the tetragrammaton, as was Metatron,
similar to the event concerning Rab Idit. A certain
heretic asked Rab Idit: 'It is written: "And to Moshe He
said 'ascend to YHWH'"[212] – it should have said "ascend
to Me"!' [Rab Idit] said to him: 'This is Metatron, whose
name is like the name of his master.' [The heretic
replied:] 'If so, then we should worship him!' [Rab Idit]
said to him: 'It is written: "Do not defy [Heb. *tammer*]

---

[211] For more, see *The Commentary of R. ḥoṭer b. Shelōmō to the
Thirteen Principles of Maimonides* (Leiden: Brill, 1974), p.91.
[212] *Exodus* 24:1.

him"[213] – [which can be used via *derasha* to mean] do not replace Me [Heb. *temireni*] with him.' [The heretic replied:] 'If so, why [does the verse continue] 'for he will not bear your trespass'? [Rab Idit] said to him: 'We hold the belief that we would not accept [Metatron] even as a messenger, as it is written: "If Your face not travel [with us], etc."[214],[215] And from this you can equate to the aforementioned *parṣufim*, which are created beings, that it is false to believe that '*abba*' creates, or '*imma*', or any of the other *parṣufim*, let alone to serve them or to direct our *tefilla* and blessings to the *ze'ir anpin* as per the *Zohar* and those who followed after it, whom [the *Zohar*] swayed with its abundant persuasions and smooth talk, like the statement of Shelomo *a"h*: 'She sways him with her abundant persuasions, and[216] with her smooth talk she pulls him in!'[217] And even to join them and unite them with our God is forbidden, as it says: 'Only to the Lord alone'![218]

Now, what his esteemed eminence wrote regarding the book *Oz Le-lohim*, whose author is Neḥemia Ḥayyun of the group of the false messiah Shabbetai Ṣebi – we also know this, and he has a further

---

[213] Ibid. 23:21.

[214] Ibid. 33:15.

[215] *bSanhedrin* 38b.

[216] The word 'and' is not present in the original *pasuq*.

[217] *Proverbs* 7:21.

[218] *Exodus* 22:19.

[commentary] on Tora called *Debar Nehemia*, [and] also the book *Hemdat Yamim* by Nathan of Gaza, prophet of Shabbetai Ṣebi's *shr"y*[219]. Rabbi Ya'aqob Sappir already wrote in his book [*Eben Sappir*], section *Hadre Teman*, that in Yemen there are books that were burned in Jerusalem – yet in Yemen they consider [them] holy;[220] his words are hinting to these three books. But indeed, we brought their words, for they are drawn from the *Zohar*! And in reality the *Zohar* is like one of [those three books], except that it is like one who removed [the husks] from on top of the storage container in order to deceive[221] and to cover up the improper beliefs, using meticulousness of other *miṣvot* and extra stringencies in

---

[219] In contrast to *zṣ"l*, this acronym stands for *shem reshaim yirqab*, 'may the name of the wicked rot'. Both expressions are found in *Proverbs* 10:7.

[220] *Eben Sappir, Hadre Teman* 28, *Yom HaShabbat Uqeriat HaTorah – Tefillatam Uminhagam*, p.61a. The full line reads: 'And here, since precious books were not widespread previously, they consider anything contained in the [books'] pages to be holy, true and correct, about which one cannot cast aspersions, as *halakha* given to Moshe at Sinai. (And even words of heresy, God forbid – if they are printed [in a text], they will not inspect after them. Even in the realm of *Kabbalah*, when I saw here the books of Nehemia Hayyun on *Kabbalah* and exposition, which we purged from the land in our countries – and yet they regard it as holy and blessed!)'

[221] This refers to the *halakha* that a seller may not remove the husks from only the top layer of grain in a storage container, as it implies that the entire container has had the husks removed and is filled with only grain, which constitutes deception. See *Mishneh Torah, Hilkhot Mekhira* 18:4.

exaggerations and hyperboles, **while intending to invalidate the *Mishnah*** – the foundation of the oral law which Moshe received from the mouth of the Almighty, and over which our rabbis *z"l* toiled in the *Talmud Babli* and *Yerushalmi* in order to explain and clarify it! The *Zohar* disgraces [the *Mishna*], calling it 'maidservant' and '*qelipa*', 'another rock that has no flowing [waters] of wisdom in it,'[222] and other degrading and demeaning terms. And [it states] that Moshe Rabbenu *a"h* was punished by being buried outside of the land of Israel, a *ṭame* land, only because he gave us the *mishnah*; [the *Zohar*] reads the following *pasuq* concerning the *mishnah*: 'On account of three things, the earth shakes ... **a maidservant who supplants her mistress'**[223] – **this is the *mishnah*.** (*Zohar Bereshit* [I] 22, top of 28[a], and [*Zohar* III] *Teṣe* 279[b] in *Ra'ya Mehemna* and *Tiqqunim*.)

Ultimately, all the words of his esteemed eminence, our teacher and rabbi, his hypotheses and theories, are flying through the air of his imagination, without the 'light of the Lord, the soul of man'[224] – [i.e.] the upright intellect which God, may He be blessed, bestowed upon humanity by which to separate between

---

[222] The metaphor draws on the incidents involving Moshe striking a rock for it to give forth water.

[223] *Proverbs* 30:22.

[224] Ibid. 20:27.

truth and falsehood, according to the Torah (that is written) and the *miṣva* (the oral law, as our rabbis *z"l* said[225]), about which is said: 'For the *miṣva* is a candle, and the Torah [is] light.'[226] Now his esteemed eminence said that 'if [we] penetrate into [his esteemed eminence's] words, [we] shall return and say: "Surely the Lord is in this place".' Now that we have penetrated into the depths of your words, our master, we have not found any reason at all; [we have] answered in direct words[227] that are clear to their foundations,[228] as is incumbent upon us: 'And you shall know today and set this to your heart [that the Lord is God in the heavens above and on the earth below; no other].'[229] And it says: 'In order that you know and have faith in me, and understand that I am He – before me, no god was formed, and after me shall no [god] be.'[230] And there are many *pesuqim* similar to the above!

Therefore, our teacher and rabbi, upon you it is incumbent to inform [us] where these new gods and *parṣufim* are mentioned, whom the kabbalists say are our God, as per the *Zohar*, and that the *'aboda* and *tefilla* [should be] to the *ze'ir anpin* specifically, even though it

---

[225] *bBerakhot* 5a.

[226] *Proverbs* 6:23.

[227] Ibid. 24:26.

[228] Paraphrasing ibid. 25:11.

[229] *Deuteronomy* 4:39.

[230] *Isaiah* 43:10.

is [a] created [being]! Upon you it is incumbent to bring a proof from the Torah, Prophets, Writings and from the words of our rabbis *z"l.*

Secondly, where in the words of our rabbis *z"l* do we find that the One who said 'let us make man' is not the same as the One who said 'let there be light' and 'let the waters be gathered' and 'let there be luminaries', as the author of the *Zohar* said?

Thirdly, why does the *Zohar* call the *ze'ir anpin* 'mighty God' – are there not *parṣufim* above it who gave it kingship, and surely the **one who gives kingship** is greater than the king, for indeed the *Zohar* explained that none of the *illot* that are the *parṣufim* can take any action without receiving permission from the *illa* that is above it? As opposed to **adam qadmon**, who said 'see now that I am indeed He, I put to death and I give life, and there is no saviour from My hand,'[231] for he alone has no one from whom he receives permission, for he is above all of them; thus it should be fitting to call him 'mighty God' and not the *ze'ir anpin*, who is smaller than he!

Fourthly, since they are created beings, how can we join them and partner them with our God who is their soul, according to their words, as they said: '"Serve

---

Him" – the *ze'ir anpin*, even though it is a created being, for you serve its soul!'[232]

Fifthly, behold our rabbis *z"l* said: 'No prophet is now permitted to invent anything.'[233] Even the double letters of *mem, nun, ṣade, pe, kaf* – which are in the middle of a word and which at the end – they said [that] 'they forgot them, then reinstated them'[234], and not that they instituted it [themselves]. Yet the author of the *Zohar* invented these *parṣufim* [to be] our God, of the name 'the holy One, blessed be He', about whom it says 'and the *atiq yomin* sat'[235] (*Zohar Bereshit* [I] 22[a])!

Sixthly, it is a clear matter that before Rabbenu HaQadosh, no work was authored [in writing] of the oral law; rather, all would review their studies and recite *mishnayyot* orally, until Rabbenu HaQadosh came and saw that the hearts[236] were diminished and that the troubles and harsh decrees had increased, and perhaps God forbid the Torah would be forgotten from Israel! Thus, he composed the *mishnah*, and he and his *bet din* relied upon the statement of the *pasuq*: '[It is] the time to

---

[232] *Vide supra* text accompanying note 54.

[233] See e.g., *bMegillah* 2b–3a.

[234] Ibid.

[235] *Daniel* 7:9.

[236] Metaphorically, the heart is viewed as the seat of understanding.

act for the Lord – they have abrogated your Torah,'[237] as HaRaMBa"M explained in his introduction to the Order of *Zeraim*. Thus the author of the *Zohar* speaks falsehood about Rabbi Shimon and his colleagues, when he said that permission was given to Elijah and all the masters of the supernal academy, and all the armies of angels in agreement to that group [to write down the *Zohar*] (Introduction to *Tiqqunim* [17a] and the ruling of Rabbi Isaac [b. Immanuel] de Lattes)!

Seventhly, the *Zohar* and the kabbalists following it validate the existence of another god, consisting of the ten *sefirot* and *parṣufim* of the *siṭra aḥra*, *mesa'aba*, *adam beliya'al* etc., and they say: 'Both of these against each other did the {most high} God make'[238] – *parṣufim* of holiness **to serve them, and *parṣufim* of the *siṭra aḥra*** [of] uncleanliness [*mesa'aba*] **to distance them**; contrary to our Torah that said that there is no other god extant in the world besides HaShem, our God, who has no beginning to His beginning!

Is HaShem in all these beliefs which are foreign to our holy written and oral Torah? Is HaShem in the belief of multiple creators, *abba* commanding *imma* to create, and she immediately fulfilling his command,

---

[237] *Psalms* 119:126. This *pasuq* is read, according to *derasha*, as: '[It is] time to act for the Lord – [therefore] they have abrogated your Torah.'

[238] *Ecclesiastes* 7:14.

except for the creation of *Adam HaRishon* whom she created without *abba*'s permission, and thus when he sinned with the tree of knowledge of good and evil, He drove him out of the Garden of Eden and drove her out with him? And the two of the, *abba* and *imma*, created the great, mighty and awesome god (according to their words), [namely] the *ze'ir anpin* who is *ben ḥakham* to both *abba* and *imma*, whom all the kabbalists serve on the advice of the author of the *Zohar*, as they explained in their books. Is HaShem in the serving of a created force, the *ze'ir anpin*, new gods, who have come about recently,[239] who are referenced in neither the written nor oral Torah?

To all of these, and similar examples, may his esteemed eminence our master set his understanding heart and intellect to bring proofs from the words of the living God, Torah, Prophets and Writings, and from the words of our rabbis *z"l*, the masters of the true *qabbala* (= tradition) which they received, general principles and specific details of the Torah, and which they handed over to us in the *mishnah* and the two talmuds, *Babli* and *Yerushalmi*, and their true *midrashim* in which there is no duplicity with clear matters, answering in direct words,[240] and not in fanciful imaginations – all for the

---

[239] Paraphrasing *Deuteronomy* 32:17.
[240] *Vide supra* n.140.

glory of our Father, our King, who bestowed humanity with knowledge to understand the veracity of true statements by the light of His perfect written and oral Torah, in accordance with the statement of the sweet one of songs of Israel: 'The laws of the Lord are true, righteous altogether.'[241]

And may the peace of your Torah, our master, make the Torah great and mighty, in accordance with his exalted soul and the soul of the one who honours you.

Yiḥya b. Suleman al-Qafiḥ

Signed:
HaRab HaGaon Yiḥya b. Salam al-Abiṣ *yṣ"w* [242]
HaRab HaGaon Salam b. Yiḥya Qaraḥ *Hy"w* [243]
HaRab HaGaon Yiḥya b. Yosef Jiat *yṣ"w*
HaRab HaGaon Raḥa b. Salam Ṣarum *yṣ"w*

◆

---

[241] *Psalms* 19:10.
[242] *yṣ"w* is an acronym for *yebarekhehu ṣureinu weyishmerehu*, 'may our Rock bless him and guard him.'
[243] *Hy"w* is an acronym for *HaShem yishmerehu*, 'may God protect him.'

About the Editor

J.J. Kimche is a PhD candidate at Harvard University, where he specialises in the intersection between European and Jewish Intellectual history during the post-Enlightenment era. He received his undergraduate education at Shalem College, Jerusalem, where he double-majored in Western philosophy and Jewish thought. Prior to that, he studied at Yeshivat Har Etzion and completed his military service in the 101st Division of the IDF's Paratroopers Brigade.

J.J. has been involved in studying and teaching Jewish ideas throughout his entire adult life. Over the past decade he has taught Jewish philosophy at various Yeshivot and schools, lectured on Greek philosophy at a pre-army academy, and taught for three years at MIT Hillel. He has taught courses in Jewish and Western intellectual history at Harvard University, Brandeis University, Case Western Reserve University, and at Gratz College.

His popular writings have been published in the *Wall Street Journal*, *First Things*, and *City Journal*. He has also published essays in a variety of academic journals, and currently serves as an editorial associate at the *Harvard Theological Review*. He has ghostwritten two books on Jewish ideas, and his first academic book is due to be published in the forthcoming year.

He may be found conversing with other scholars on the *Podcast of Jewish Ideas*, which he hosts.

About Da'at Press

Da'at Press is dedicated to publishing works from Jewish scholars of the past, present, and future.

To find out more about our books and online learning community, please visit www.daat.press and www.thehabura.com

Made in United States
Orlando, FL
21 September 2024

51631914R00114